DAWNING OF THE DINOSAURS

THE STORY OF CANADA'S OLDEST DINOSAURS

By Harry Thurston
Illustrated by Ivan Murphy

Co-published by
NIMBUS PUBLISHING LIMITED
and
THE NOVA SCOTIA MUSEUM
Halifax, Nova Scotia
1994

94 95 96 97 98 99 8 7 6 5 4 3 2 1

Produced by the Nova Scotia Museum as part of the
Education Resource Services Program of the
Department of Education, Province of Nova Scotia

Minister: The Honourable John D. MacEachern
Deputy Minister: Robert P. Moody

A collaborative project of the Nova Scotia Museum,
the Cumberland Development Authority and
the Fundy Geological Museum

Co-published by the Nova Scotia Museum and
Nimbus Publishing Limited

A product of the Nova Scotia Co-publishing Program

Illustrations:
Ivan Murphy

Design and typographic formatting:
David H. MacDonald

Cover Imagesetting:
Nova Scotia Digital Technologies Ltd., Halifax

Imagesetting, Film and Printing:
McCurdy Printing and Typesetting Ltd., Halifax

Main text set in Bembo 11/12

Canadian Cataloguing in Publication Data
Thurston, Harry, 1950
Dawning of the dinosaurs, (Peeper)
Co-published by the Nova Scotia Museum
ISBN 1–55109–100–3

1. Dinosaurs–Nova Scotia. i. Nova Scotia Museum.
ii. Title. iii. Series

QE862.D5148 1994 567.9'1'09716 C94-950119-0

CONTENTS

ACKNOWLEDGEMENTS

The author gratefully acknowledges the generous support of the Cumberland Development Authority without which the research and writing of this book would not have been possible. He extends a special thanks to Jonathan Nicols and Pam Harrison for their confidence and patience.

The author also would like to thank the many persons who gave generously of their time and expertise: Paul Olsen, Lamont-Doherty Geological Observatory of Columbia University; Hans-Dieter Sues, Royal Ontario Museum; Robert Grantham, Curator, Geology, Nova Scotia Museum; Ken Adams, Curator, Fundy Geological Museum; Neil Shubin, University of Pennsylvania; Eldon George, Parrsboro, Nova Scotia; Don Reid, Joggins, Nova Scotia; Laing Ferguson, Mt. Allison University.

As well, the author thanks the creative and editorial team that contributed to the development of the book: John Hennigar-Shuh, Curator, Publications, Nova Scotia Museum; Debra Burleson, Manager of Interpretation, Education, Nova Scotia Museum; Etta Moffatt, Nova Scotia Museum; Ken Adams, Fundy Geological Museum and Robbie Rudnicki, technical editor.

The author offers kudos to the illustrator Ivan Murphy and book designer David MacDonald, with whom it was a pleasure to work.

The author thanks the following for permission to quote passages: Simon & Schuster Inc., from *Kings of Creation* by Don Lessem; The Reader's Digest Association (Canada) Ltd., from *"Parrsboro's Fabulous Fossils"* by Mark Walters, which appeared in the February 1988 issue of Reader's Digest.

Drawings for Wasson Bluff Walk used by permission from Roy Shlische of Rutgers University and Paul Olsen.

Dedicated with love to my daughter Meaghan

A TROVE OF FOSSILS

In January 1986, Paul Olsen of Columbia University's Lamont-Doherty Geological Observatory and Neil H. Shubin of Harvard University made a headline-grabbing announcement from the National Geographic Society's headquarters in Washington, D.C. On the shores of the Bay of Fundy, the youthful team had uncovered the biggest fossil find in North America from a critical period in earth history, 200 million years ago (mya)—the time when dinosaurs were emerging as the dominant land animals.

From three tons of earth Olsen and Shubin, with colleague Hans-Dieter Sues of the Smithsonian Institution, had collected 100 000 fossilized bones, belonging to ancestral crocodiles, lizards, sharks, primitive fishes, and large and small dinosaurs. Among this trove of fossils were the oldest dinosaurs—by some 70 million years—ever found in Canada. Some of the most intriguing dinosaur fossils were not bones at all but trackways left by the long-extinct "terrible lizards." Among them was a set of three-toed footprints about the size of a penny—the smallest dinosaur tracks ever found. This unique discovery had been made not by professional paleontologists but by amateur fossil collector Eldon George of Parrsboro, Nova Scotia.

Bones were recovered from ancient river channels, sand dunes, and basalt (lava) talus heaps, where, Shubin said, they were splattered like "bits in Rocky Road ice cream." Among the fragments, however, were two perfectly preserved skulls of lizard-like **sphenodontids** and the first complete jaw bones of **trithelodonts**, very rare reptiles most closely related to mammals. The vertebrate animals found near Parrsboro offered a critical insight into the world as we know it. With the exception of dinosaurs, the same groups are living today: fishes, crocodiles, turtles, frogs, salamanders, and mammals. In Shubin's opinion, the Parrsboro fossils presented a picture of "the modern world in embryo."

It was not the first time that the Bay of Fundy's coastal cliffs had yielded an epoch-marking discovery of world importance. In 1851, Sir Charles Lyell, the Scottish-born founder of modern geology, and Sir William Dawson, a native Nova Scotian who founded McGill University of Montreal, discovered in the fossil tree trunks of Joggins, Nova Scotia, the remains of the first terrestrial reptile. Even though this tiny, ancient forest dweller lived in the Carboniferous Period, 100 million years before dinosaurs trod the earth, it was the true ancestor of the "terrible lizards."

These discoveries have established the Bay of Fundy as one of the classic fossil localities in the Western Hemisphere. It is remarkable that two sites—100 million years apart in time but separated by only 40 kilometres (25 miles)—should cast light on two of the most important chapters in paleontological history: the evolution of vertebrates onto land, and the beginning of the Age of Dinosaurs.

The Bay of Fundy fossil discoveries address a number of other critical questions in paleontology. For example, what was the nature of early mammals? Were dinosaurs cold- or warm-blooded? And not least, what global catastrophes led to the rise and eventual demise of the dinosaurs? These are some of the questions that this book will explore, in addition to telling the story of how dinosaurs came to rule the earth for 140 million years.

FOSSILS OF FUNDY

Very few dinosaurs, or other extinct animals, that once lived on Earth have been preserved as fossils—perhaps a small fraction of one percent. Even so, fossils are found from all stages of an animal's life and present a picture of the full range of its activities—from birth to death.

There are two basic types of fossils. First, there are body fossils, which are remains of the animal's carcass. Second, there are trace fossils, so-called because they are traces of the activities of the living animal. The most common examples of the latter are footprints or trackways. Body fossils are generally less common than trackways.

Often, conditions that favour one type of preservation are less than ideal for the other. Therefore, it is uncommon to have both trace fossils and body fossils from the same site. Fundy is exceptional in that it has both body and trace fossils in abundance.

Fossils require special conditions for preservation, which explains why they are so rare. In the Fundy basin, both trace and body fossils were buried by water-borne sediments pouring down from the Cobequid Mountains, or in some instances by migrating sand dunes. Millions of years later, these deeply buried sediments were uplifted by events that are still poorly understood. Today, the elements and the erosive power of the Fundy tides continue to expose this trove of fossils.

TRACKWAYS

The most abundant trace fossils in Fundy are footprints and trackways. They were left in muddy sediments along the shores of a seasonal lake that occupied the Fundy basin, 200 million years ago. *(See Chapter 4).*

FEEDING TRACES

Scraps of meals and bones bearing teeth marks are called feeding traces. Leftovers of ancient lunches have been found in Fundy.

SKIN IMPRINTS

Skin imprints have been found in association with trackways. They are considered trace fossils as they likely were left by living animals.

COPROLITES

Coprolites, thought to be the droppings of dinosaurs or crocodiles, have also been found. They offer insights into the diets of these ancient animals.

EGGS AND NESTS

Fundy has yet to yield dinosaur eggs. For unknown reasons, dinosaur eggs are very rare in Triassic- and Jurassic-age sediments.

GASTROLITHS

Rare gastroliths, or stomach stones, have been found in association with the rib cages of a herbivorous prosauropod dinosaur. It probably used these polished, rounded stones for grinding up plant matter, in the same way as modern birds employ grit in their gizzards.

ANATOMICAL REMAINS

Usually these are hard parts of the anatomy, such as bones and teeth. But soft body parts, such as skin and cartilage, may occasionally be preserved. Normally, scavengers clean the flesh from the dead animals' bones, and bacteria and the elements begin to break down and wear away the bones themselves. However, in rare instances, the animal may be partially preserved if the carcass is in water and is covered by silt, or, if on land, is buried under sand. In both instances, oxygen is prevented from reaching the carcass, which slows the decomposition process. As sediment builds up, minerals in water may be deposited in the pore spaces of the bone, or the bone tissue itself may be replaced by crystals. Either way, the bones are "petrified," or turned to stone.

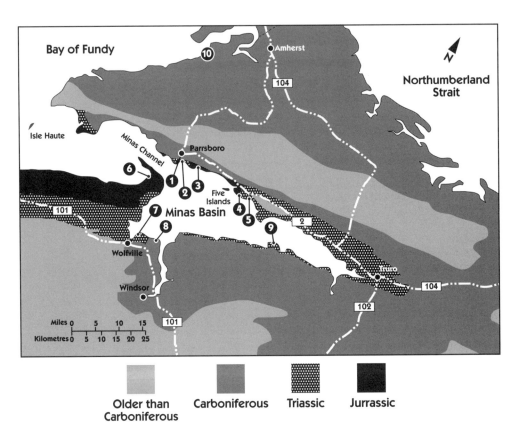

FOSSIL LOCATIONS OF FUNDY

1 **Parrsboro:** Fern imprints, brachiopods, corals, amphibian tracks

2 **Wasson Bluff:** Trithelodont and dinosaur bones; fish, crocodile, lizard, shark remains

3 **Moose River:** Fern imprints, tree trunks, arthropod tracks

4 **Carrs Brook:** Plant fossils, amphibians, reptiles

5 **Economy:** Dinosaur bones

6 **Scots Bay:** Fish, dinosaur footprints, reptiles, snails, clams, plant fossils

7 **Evangeline Beach:** Dinosaurs, rhyncosaurs, mammal-like reptiles, aetosaurs

8 **Horton Bluff:** Amphibian tracks

9 **Burntcoat Head:** Dinosaurs, amphibians, mammal-like reptiles, aetosaurs

10 **Joggins:** Ferns, tree trunks, snails, amphibians, reptiles, arthropod tracks

CHAPTER ONE

WHEN DINOSAURS BEGAN TO RULE THE EARTH

*What makes these fossils most remarkable is that here, as virtually
nowhere else on earth, it is possible not only to find unusual dinosaurs
but to locate their place in time with impressive exactness.*

DON LESSEM, 1992

KINGS OF CREATION

n 1970, a budding paleontologist from New Jersey, Paul Olsen, was walking through a driving rain along the north shore of the Minas Basin. He had come to Nova Scotia, knowing the Triassic sediments presented a chance to uncover early dinosaurs. He had sleuthed the Five Islands area and found some bone fragments and fish fossils. He was now working up the cliffs from Moose River to Wasson Bluff. It was October; the rain was cold. He hunched deeper into his raincoat and tried to keep his umbrella—a sheet of plastic—positioned over the clipboard which held his soggy map. His eyes were downcast as he plodded along with an almost numb doggedness. Then, on the beach in front of him, he saw fragments of fossilized bone that apparently had been washed from the cliff by the torrential rain.

Jubilant, Olsen returned to his field camp eager to show his prize. He was working with Donald Baird, his mentor from Princeton University, and Jack Horner, a Princeton preparator who a few years later would achieve worldwide fame for his discovery of a nest and hatchlings of duckbill dinosaurs in Montana. That night he watched as the more experienced men pieced together a neck vertebra. The size of the vertebra pegged it as that of a medium-sized **prosauropod**, a long-necked dinosaur with a small head, that could attain a length of 4 metres (13 feet).

The dinosaur walked a world alien to the one travelled by Olsen. The sun beat down mercilessly on this ancient traveller. Probably it travelled in company with other herbivorous (plant-eating) **prosauropods**. They passed through a desiccated region of sulphate soils (the remains of dried-up saline lakes) and reddish sand dunes swept into crescent shapes by the dry, prevailing northwest wind. The Fundy Basin then resembled Death Valley in California. In very many ways, the prosauropods were like camels in a desert. Shallow lakes (playa) lay far off where they were fed by seasonal streams spilling down from the mountains, which today are the eroded Cobequids—mountains in name only.

Olsen could see this living landscape in the frozen layers of stone that wall in the Bay of Fundy. Over the next decade, he would decipher the complicated geology of the rocks near Parrsboro. He concluded that many rock formations were not Triassic, as geologists had long believed, but Jurassic in age. This proved a critical insight that set the stage for the important fossil discoveries to follow.

ON THE SHORES OF A NEW AGE

Standing on the north shore of the Minas Basin, at Parrsboro, you are in the midst of some of the finest seaside scenery Nova Scotia has to offer. Dominating the seascape is the great red headland of Blomidon, standing out against the sky. Between Parrsboro and Blomidon, the world's highest tides flood through the Minas Channel, twice daily rising and falling 12 to 15 metres, and eroding the soft sandstone that borders the upper Bay of Fundy. A well-travelled observer might note that the reddish, steep wave-cut cliffs and flat-topped mountains are similar in appearance to the mesas of the southwestern United States, in particular the Arizona desert region. In fact, the sediments were deposited at about the same time, during the Triassic and Jurassic Periods, 248-201 million years ago (mya).

The Newark Supergroup of Eastern North America

Key to Basins:

1 Wadesboro Subbasin of Deep River Basin
2 Sanford Subbasin of Deep River Basin
3 Durham Subbasin of Deep River Basin
4 Davie County Basin
5 Dan River – Danville Basin
6 Scottsburg Basin
7 Briery Creek Basin and subsidiary basin to the south
8 Farmville Basin
9 Richmond Basin
10 Exposed part of Taylorsville Basin
11 Scotsville Basin
12 Culpeper Basin
13 Gettysburg Basin
14 Newark Basin
15 Pomperaug Basin
16 Hartford Basin
17 Deerfield Basin
18 Fundy Basin

At the beginning of the Triassic period, Nova Scotia was located near the equator in the middle of a single super-continent known as **Pangaea**, or "One Earth." Wedged between present-day Africa and North America, it was far from the moderating influence of the ocean. There was no Bay of Fundy, no Gulf of St. Lawrence, no Atlantic Ocean. The climate was harshly continental, hot and dry, punctuated by intermittent, sometimes heavy, rains.

Then, in the Late Triassic (225 mya), the Earth entered a period of great change. The crust weakened and the continental plates began to pull apart to form what is now the Atlantic Ocean. The plates ruptured along fault lines roughly parallel to the present-day continental margin of the Eastern Seaboard. Rift valleys, similar to East Africa's Great Rift Valley, formed as blocks subsided along fault lines from Nova Scotia to South Carolina. These valleys become sedimentary basins known as the **Newark Supergroup**, of which Fundy is the largest and most northerly.

Throughout the Triassic, sediments continued to fill in these basins. In Fundy, rains of monsoon intensity swelled rivers that carried coarse sediments from the Nova Scotia highlands into the basin. Later, lakes occupied the basin floor and finer bottom sediments piled up to impressive thicknesses—up to 1 000 metres (3 000 ft) in total.

As the Jurassic Age succeeded the Triassic (208 mya), the continental rifting process became more intense, further stressing the already weakened crust. Molten magma spewed from fissures in fiery lava fountains and spread over the red sandstones. Today, this lava appears as dark basalt capping headlands near Parrsboro and forming the tabletop of the North Mountain, which stretches for 200 km (125 miles) from Blomidon to Brier Island. Alternating dry and wet cycles continued into the Jurassic, depositing sandstones and siltstones on top of the basalt.

This tumultuous time in earth history formed the setting for the evolution of the dinosaurs. Near the juncture where the intense red sandstones meet the sombre greys of basalt, the dinosaurs seized the day. They would not relinquish supremacy for another 140 million years, at the end of the Cretaceous Period.

DATING THE ROCKS

Life on the planet is divided into three main Eras: Paleozoic, Mesozoic, and Cenozoic. Mesozoic means "the era of middle animals." The Mesozoic itself was divided into three major periods: Triassic, Jurassic, and Cretaceous. These names derive from so-called "type" sediments which were first described in classic geological studies and later applied universally to all rocks of the same age. The Triassic was based on sediments in Germany, the Jurassic on marine limestones from the Jura Mountains in France, and the Cretaceous on white chalks (Latin *creta*), visible in the cliffs along the English channel. Geologists date rocks by both direct and indirect methods.

More than 180 years ago, the first geologists to study Earth history worked out a system that is still used. Sedimentary rocks, such as sandstones, mudstones, and limestones, are laid down in layers known as beds or strata, giving the appearance of a layer cake. According to this "layer cake" principle, the oldest rocks are on the bottom and the most recent at the top. Geologists assume that fossils found in a given layer lived during the period that the rock was being laid down. The presence of certain animal or plant fossils in a rock stratum become tags to identify it as being of a certain age. This system, known as **biostratigraphy**, can then be applied universally. If the same fossils appear in widely separated rocks, they can safely be said to be the same age. Therefore, the age of rocks in Canada, say, can be compared to that of rocks in England.

Biostratigraphy, however, only gives us relative ages of the rocks. More recently, scientists have devised a geochemical means called **radiometry** to measure the absolute ages of rock. It is based on the fact that certain radioactive elements, such as uranium and potassium, occur in an unstable condition. These elements are said to decay. As they do so they give off radioactivity and, in the process, are transformed into another element. For example, potassium-40 becomes argon-40.

Era	Duration (Millions of years)	Period	Duration (Millions of years)	Millions of Years Ago	Evolution of life as recorded by fossils
Cenozoic	65	Quaternary	3	3	Origin and evolution of humans
		Tertiary	63		Evolution of mammals
				66	Extinction of dinosaurs
Mesozoic	160	Cretaceous	78		**Zenith of dinosaurs** Bony fishes Flowering plants
				144	
		Jurassic	57		First birds **Development of giant dinosaurs** **Parrsboro**
				201	
		Triassic	44		**First Dinosaurs** - First mammals
				245	Wide extinctions
Paleozoic	345	Permian	41		Dominance of mammal-like reptiles
				286	
		(Pennsylvanian) Carboniferous (Mississippian)	74		**Joggins** First reptiles Dominance of amphibians
				360	
		Devonian	48		First amphibians Air-breathing fishes Primitive land plants
				408	
		Silurian	30		First jawed fishes First land-living animals
				438	
		Ordovician	67		Jawless fishes
				505	
		Cambrian	65		First vertebrates Invertebrates widely established Appearance of numerous fossils
				570	
		"Precambrian"	4000		Fossils rare Algae Origin of Earth

The time it takes for half of the radioactive element to decay into another element is called the "half-life" of the element and can be calculated precisely. Only certain kinds of rock, such as lava, can be dated radiometrically. Fortunately, in Fundy, there are abundant lava flows for radiometric dating. Using the potassium-argon method, North Mountain basalt has been dated at 201±1 million years, that is, the time of the earliest Jurassic. The lava flow also helps to date the layers of sedimentary rocks above and below it. Anything above it must be Jurassic in age.

CLOCK IN THE CLIFF

In Fundy, geologists are able to fine-tune the dating to an even more precise degree. Due to astronomical cycles, called Van Houten cycles, climatic changes occurred regularly on a 21 000-year basis, shifting from times of monsoon rains to dry periods. The monsoons resulted in the formation of large ancient lakes in the rift valleys, similar to Lake Baikal in Asia and Lake Tanganyika in Africa which today occupy rift valleys. At the end of the cycle, there was a shift in monsoon rain patterns to the other hemisphere and the lakes tended to dry up, leaving salt deposits. These salt layers are clearly visible as light-coloured bands in the sedimentary cliffs bordering the Bay of Fundy. Using this clock in the cliff, the geologist can quickly click through geological time at 21 000-year intervals.

The Fundy rocks, then, can be dated by both standard methods, biostratigraphy and radiometry, and with the further aid of the lake cycles, the age of the fossils can be determined very precisely. This precision greatly enhances the importance of the Fundy fossil discoveries.

ROSETTA STONE OF THE EARLY JURASSIC

Neil Shubin called the Jurassic-age sediments along the Fundy coastline "a Rosetta Stone," after the famous tablet used to decipher ancient Egyptian writing. What did he mean?

In Shubin's opinion, the most important aspect of the Fundy find is that the fossils are the first from a known earliest Jurassic locality. Until Olsen confirmed the age of the Fundy basin rocks, there were no early Jurassic fossils in North America that could be dated with accuracy. In paleontological circles, it was referred to as the "case of the missing earliest Jurassic." The abundant well-dated Fundy fossils give us a first glimpse into a previously unknown time in our geological history.

In Fundy there are many of lines of evidence with which to date the rocks: tracks, pollen, fossil plants, fossil vertebrates, radiometric dates, and astronomical cycles. (Any two would normally be considered good.) Fundy fossils now can be used to understand Jurassic localities in other places, such as China and Africa, that are not as rich in sources of evidence.

In Fundy—as nowhere else—you can see the dawning of the Age of Dinosaurs. Standing on the north shore of the Minas Basin, beside the coastal cliffs of Jurassic age at Wasson Bluff, near Parrsboro, looking across the turbulent waters of the Minas Channel to the brilliant red Triassic bluff of Blomidon, Paul Olsen could declare: "This is the only place where you can see the change in the animal assemblage through that critical time when dinosaurs began to rule the earth. On the other shore, they didn't rule the earth yet, and here, they did."

CHAPTER TWO

RISE OF THE REPTILES

"...I rose early next morning, and taking some luncheon in my basket, walked along the shore... The tide favoured my expedition, and the day was fine, though small banks of fog drifted up the bay from time to time, dissolving as they touched the cliffs, warmed by the sun. I returned in the evening to the quarrymen's shanty, thoroughly fatigued, but loaded with fossils, delighted with the knowledge I had acquired, and with my enthusiasm for geology raised to a higher point than ever before..."

SIR WILLIAM DAWSON

AN AUTOBIOGRAPHY, FIFTY YEARS IN SCIENCE, 1890

ore than likely, fog is drifting up the Bay today, dissolving against the now-famous fossil cliffs at Joggins, just as it did in Dawson's day.

At Joggins, when you descend the seaside stairway to the beach and turn right, to the northeast, you are following in the footsteps of two of paleontology's pioneers. A century and a half ago, they were on the verge of a discovery that was to secure for Joggins an important place in our understanding of how life evolved on Earth.

In 1852, Charles Lyell, author of the multivolume textbook *Principles of Geology*, was en route to Boston to give the Lowell Lectures. He had written his friend Sir William Dawson, author of the regional classic *Acadian Geology*, telling him: "I should like very much to exchange ideas and to geologize with you for a few days from Halifax to St. John."

Their prime destination was Joggins, which had so impressed Lyell on his first trip to Nova Scotia, a decade before.

Lyell's guide had been Abraham Gesner, doctor and geologist, who gained fame as the inventor of kerosene. Gesner had waxed eloquent about the riches of the Joggins shore "on which broken trunks and limbs of ancient trees are scattered in great profusion—the place where the delicate herbage of a former world is now transmuted into stone."

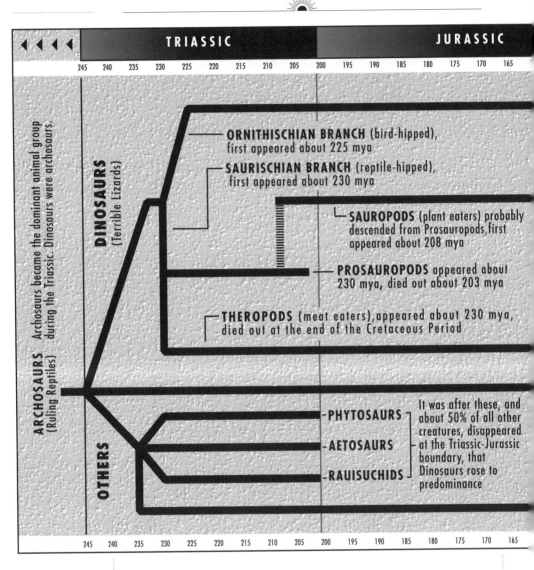

ARCHOSAURS (Ruling Reptiles) — Archosaurs became the dominant animal group during the Triassic. Dinosaurs were archosaurs.

DINOSAURS (Terrible Lizards)

ORNITHISCHIAN BRANCH (bird-hipped), first appeared about 225 mya

SAURISCHIAN BRANCH (reptile-hipped), first appeared about 230 mya

SAUROPODS (plant eaters) probably descended from Prosauropods, first appeared about 208 mya

PROSAUROPODS appeared about 230 mya, died out about 203 mya

THEROPODS (meat eaters), appeared about 230 mya, died out at the end of the Cretaceous Period

OTHERS

-PHYTOSAURS

-AETOSAURS

-RAUISUCHIDS

It was after these, and about 50% of all other creatures, disappeared at the Triassic-Jurassic boundary, that Dinosaurs rose to predominance

The beach still yields abundant plant fossils from the Carboniferous Period, which are constantly being quarried from the cliffs by the natural forces of ice, wind, and waves. The imprints of branches, roots, fronds, and leaves show as coaly impressions against the grey background of sandstone and shales. On occasion an entire fossilized root or cylinder of stem bark is found.

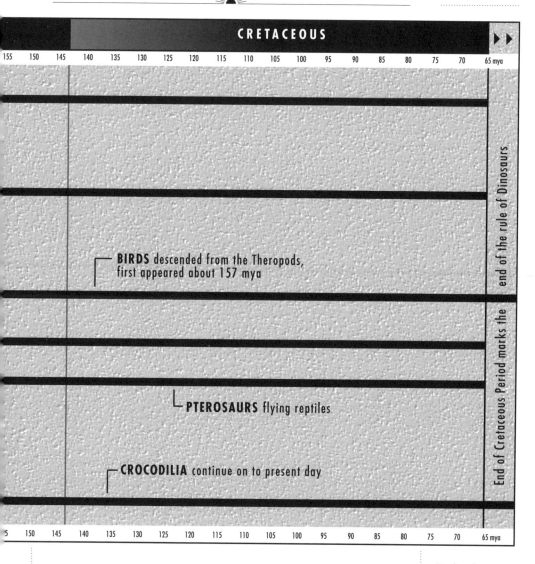

| 155 | 150 | 145 | 140 | 135 | 130 | 125 | 120 | 115 | 110 | 105 | 100 | 95 | 90 | 85 | 80 | 75 | 70 | 65 mya |

BIRDS descended from the Theropods,
first appeared about 157 mya

PTEROSAURS flying reptiles

CROCODILIA continue on to present day

end of the rule of Dinosaurs

End of Cretaceous Period marks the

| 5 | 150 | 145 | 140 | 135 | 130 | 125 | 120 | 115 | 110 | 105 | 100 | 95 | 90 | 85 | 80 | 75 | 70 | 65 mya |

Timeline showing the main groups of creatures discussed in this book

What Dawson and Lyell uncovered that August day, however, was totally unexpected. Having reached Coal Mine Point, the first prominent headland jutting into the Cumberland Basin, they kneeled to examine a pile of "fossil grindstones." Dawson knew that these cross sections of ancient trees often contained the imprint of smaller plants that had fallen into hollow tree trunks and been preserved by the pouring-in of sandy sediments. This day, another shape showed itself. The limb·bone of a vertebrate suddenly came into focus. It proved to be the first evidence that land animals had lived during the Coal Age. Until then scientists had believed that only fishes and amphibians dwelled in the Coal Age swamp. Appropriately, Dawson named the little reptile **Hylonomus**, meaning "forest dweller."

FIRST LIFE ON LAND

Until 350 million years ago, at the beginning of the Carboniferous Period, all life was waterbound. Fish were the first vertebrates—that is, backboned creatures like ourselves. A backbone gave them more mobility than other aquatic life, such as crabs which carried their skeletons on the outside. Eventually, fish developed air-breathing lungs and lobe-like fins that served as primitive legs, allowing them to venture onto land for short periods to feed on snails or vegetation that fringed their watery habitat. This was the beginning of what we know as the amphibious life-style.

The first amphibians, like modern-day salamanders and frogs, were tied to the water by their need to lay eggs there. Protected only by a thin membrane, their eggs would quickly dry out in the sun. As well, their skin was moist and sun-sensitive, allowing them to make only brief forays onto land.

The first vertebrates fully adapted to life on land were reptiles. Reptiles emerged about 300 million years ago, in the Pennsylvanian Period of the Carboniferous Period, and eventually gave rise to dinosaurs, modern-day crocodiles and lizards, as well as mammals. Among the earliest examples of this type of animal was *Hylonomus,* discovered by Dawson and Lyell at Joggins.

Hylonomus differed in a number of significant ways from its amphibian ancestors. Its skeleton was more robust and its limb girdles stronger to aid mobility on land. Also, its skin was dry. But the critical difference was that its eggs had a leathery protective shell. This adaptation freed it from the need to complete its reproductive cycle in the water environment. Eggs developed inside the reptile's body and were laid on land.

AIR BREATHERS OF THE COAL PERIOD

In his book, *Air Breathers of the Coal Period*, Dawson showed how *Hylonomus*, in order for it to get trapped inside a tree trunk, had to be a truly terrestrial creature. The **Lycopod** trees, which were giant relatives of the living Club mosses, grew along river channels on a flood plain. When in flood the rivers crested their banks, depositing a layer of mud over the roots of the trees, killing them. A windstorm eventually snapped off the trunks. The soft inner tissues of the tree rotted; however, the bark was durable, creating a hollow stump. With each new flood, soil accumulated around the base of the dead tree until it reached the lip of the hollow trunk, or "strange repository" to use Dawson's phrase. Unsuspecting, the little reptile came scurrying along the forest floor—and down he went, never to climb out. The next spate brought sediment pouring into the tree trunk, preserving the trapped animal. Because of this strange mechanism of capture, we know that the Joggins tree-stump fauna were land animals. Dawson originally called them **microsaurs**, meaning "little reptiles." Some, in fact, were amphibians. *Hylonomus*, however, was a true ancestral reptile. It would give rise, 100 million years later, to the "terrible lizards"—dinosaurs.

Cutaway drawing, showing *Hylonomus* trapped in the hollow stump of a rotten tree trunk

Among the skeletal remains that Dawson and Lyell disinterred from the hollow tree trunks at Joggins were those of a primitive amphibian. Dawson named it **Dendrerpeton acadianum**—after the Greek word for tree and its place of origin, Nova Scotia, once called Acadia.

All 100 specimens of **Dendrerpeton** subsequently discovered at Joggins were found in tree trunks. In 1988, however, a team of scientists from McGill University uncovered a complete skeleton in grey siltstone on the Joggins beach. It appeared the Coal Age creature had been trapped in sediments when an ancient river flooded its banks.

Not only was its method of preservation unique, it was also the first complete skeleton of this important ancient animal which was the ancestor of many amphibians and probably gave rise to modern frogs.

Dendrerpeton lived when amphibians were the dominant land animals, and reptiles, like *Hylonomus*, were just beginning to appear. A rather sluggish, cold-blooded animal, it nevertheless was capable of getting around on land.

As an adult, it reached lengths of 1 metre (3.2 feet) and would have resembled a large salamander. Its teeth tell us that it was a carnivore. Dawson speculated that it might have preyed upon fishes and smaller reptiles, but it probably scavenged many meals and fed upon the many large insects in the Coal Age swamps and forests.

Dendrerpeton, an amphibian

The largest animal at Joggins was neither a reptile nor an amphibian but an arthropod—an invertebrate with a hard jointed exoskeleton. **Arthropleura** attained a length of nearly two metres. Its trackways can often be seen at Joggins. They look like they were made by a small caterpillar tractor, as they weave in sinuous lines across slabs of Carboniferous age sediments. *Arthropleura* had a segmented body and many legs, perhaps as many as 30 pairs. It probably most resembled a giant sowbug, or wood louse, found today in damp places such as under rocks and rotting wood. Its large size probably meant that it had few, if any, enemies. The giant "bug" itself fed on the dead wood of fallen lycopod trees, and therefore played an important role in the forest ecosystem by recycling the abundant litter of the forest floor.

As giant sowbugs wound a path through the stands of bamboo-like ***Calamites***, giant dragonflies known as ***Meganeura*** flitted in and out of the light slanting through the dense foliage of the Coal Age forest. In a time when there were no birds, they were the top flying predators. Like today they were seen near water, at the edges of ponds, lakes and swamps. These ancient predators were more formidable than their modern-day counterparts, however. They had more massive jaws and much stronger and longer legs. The strong legs allowed them to snatch prey from perches. Most impressive was their wingspan, which attained breadths of 70 cm (2.5 feet)—comparable to modern-day birds of prey. These were truly dragons of the air.

Arthropleura

Mayflies shared the skies with dragonflies. They also were large compared to their modern-day descendants. They had wingspans of 10 cm (4 inches), and, unlike modern mayflies, they had strong biting mouth parts which allowed them to feed. Their large strong jaws bore teeth, suggesting that they were predatory. Larger ones may have preyed upon tadpoles of small and medium-sized amphibians.

Calamites

In 1989, amateur fossil collector Don Reid found a beautifully preserved specimen of a mayfly at Joggins. The slab of sandstone bears the imprints of raindrops—evidence of the weather that day—and the death throes of the insect. It appears that the mayfly got trapped on the sticky surface and was beating its wings in a vain effort to free itself. Such a fossil (called a **tapoglyph**) preserves the behavior of a dying animal and offers a rare insight into the world of 300 million years ago.

AGE OF REPTILES

During the late Carboniferous, two main lines of terrestrial vertebrates developed: reptiles, which led to present-day lizards, snakes, and crocodiles; and mammal-like reptiles, which gave rise to mammals.

It is surprising to learn that mammal-like reptiles actually rose to dominance first. Later, however, they went into decline for reasons that still are not fully understood. True mammals, the descendants of the once diverse mammal-like reptiles, then had to bide their time—timidly in the shadows—while the long reign of the reptiles, particularly the dinosaurs, played itself out.

The earliest mammal-like reptiles were **pelycosaurs** ("sail-reptiles"). The oldest known specimen was found in Late Carboniferous rocks at Florence, near Sydney, Nova Scotia. Other Coal Age pelycosaurs also have been found at Joggins.

During the Permian Period (290-245 mya) that followed the Coal Age, mammal-like reptiles became the dominant land animals. Nova Scotia has no rocks of Permian age, but the red rocks of neighbouring Prince Edward Island date to the Permian. They have yielded a specimen of a pelycosaur similar, if not identical, to the Permian's top predator, *Dimetrodon*. A large creature with fang-like front teeth, it had a distinctive fan-like sail on its back, which it deployed to shed heat and thus regulate its internal temperature.

The first blow to the mammal-like reptiles came 245 million years ago, when the largest mass extinction in the

Dimetrodon, an early mammal-like reptile

fossil record brought the Permian to an abrupt close. It also brought the curtain down on the Paleozoic ("Old Life") and ushered in the world of the Mesozoic ("Middle Life"), sometimes called *The Age of Reptiles*.

The Triassic, the first period of the Mesozoic Era, saw a great diversification of reptile types. Many of this cast of reptilian characters are found in Fundy. The Triassic paved the way for the 140-million-year reign of the dinosaurs that spanned the final two periods of the Mesozoic, the Jurassic and Cretaceous.

But, as the Mesozoic opened, mammal-like reptiles still held sway on land. More advanced types had replaced their primitive cousins, the pelycosaurs, as the dominant land animals. These were the **dicynodonts** (two dog teeth) and **cynodonts** (dog teeth). The oldest Mesozoic rocks in Fundy (235 mya) contain remains of dicynodont mammal-like reptiles. Dicynodonts were bulky plant eaters, ranging from pig- to rhino-size. They had horny bills, much like turtles, for grinding up plant matter, and many of them had two large canine teeth projecting from their upper jaw—thus their name. They probably used their teeth purely for display rather than food grubbing. According to Olsen, they looked like "Volkswagen Beetles with tusks."

The other major group of mammal-like reptiles, the cynodonts, gradually grew in importance. Many cynodonts were sabre-toothed carnivores that preyed upon their dicynodont

cousins. Others were herbivores, such as ***Arctotraversodont***, found near Burntcoat
Head in Late Triassic–age
rocks. This was a massive
animal, about the size of a grizzly
bear with an appropriate bear-size
jaw. Overall, however, this four-
legged animal would have most
resembled a bulky pig.

*A mammal-like
reptile similar to the
cynodont,
Arctotraversodont*

A variety of sometimes bizarre reptiles shared the Triassic with
these lumbering mammal-like reptiles. Among them was a
globally widespread and numerous group, the **procolophonids**.
Small animals, 0.6 metre (2 feet) maximum, they were
nevertheless heavily built, resembling, according to Hans-Dieter
Sues, "reptiles on steroids." The procolophonid *Hypsognathus* was
uncovered on Paddy's Island near Wolfville. It was 0.3 metre
(1 foot) long, had a broad head, bristling with horns, enormous
keyhole-shaped eyes, and, for an added touch of eccentricity,
buck teeth. Procolophonids have been described as "horned toads
of the Triassic." In fact, they may have been ancestral to turtles.

THE ARCHOSAURS TAKE OVER

At the beginning of the
Late Triassic—the period
represented in Fundy—a major
changeover of creatures took place. There was a proliferation
of a spectacular reptile group called **archosaurs** or "ruling
reptiles." As their name suggests, they became the dominant
land animals, replacing the once-powerful mammal-like
reptiles in the Triassic hierarchy. The archosaurs include the
extinct dinosaurs and **pterosaurs** as well as the ancestors of
living crocodiles. The relationship between these archosaur
groups is far from clear, although some are obviously more
primitive than others.

Archosaur-like creatures had been around for some time before the sudden upswing in their fortunes in the Late Triassic. Among the primitive archosaur-like creatures was *Tanystropheus*. It sported a neck twice the length of its body and could reach lengths of 7 metres (22 feet). Paleontologists have speculated that it may have used its outlandish neck as a kind of fishing rod. It had short limbs and must have been a partially aquatic creature in order to support the weight of its outsize neck. Measuring 30 cm (1 foot) in length, vertebrae of this creature are unmistakable. Samples were found at Carr's Brook, near Economy, N.S.

Another primitive group related to archosaurs was the **rhyncosaurs**. In fact, they were the most common and widespread reptiles in the Middle Triassic. Not surprisingly, they, too, are known from Fundy, though from the Late Triassic. These pig-like creatures, found at Evangeline Beach, possessed a long, overhanging beak which was probably used to crop vegetation.

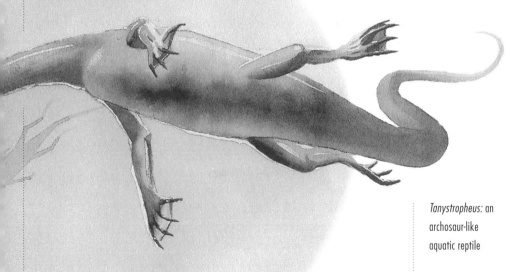

Tanystropheus: an archosaur-like aquatic reptile

Some animals that we recognize as archosaurs—at best, a "ragbag" group—resembled heavily built, long-legged crocodiles. These "gatorlizards"—to use the term coined by

Dale Russell, of Canada's National Museum of Nature—included phytosaurs, aetosaurs, and rauisuchids. All are represented in the Late Triassic of Fundy.

Phytosaurs were large aquatic reptiles (up to 6 metres, 20 feet, in length) that looked very similar to the gavial crocodiles indigenous to India. They had very long, narrow snouts, ideally suited for snatching fish. Their nostrils were located on a mound above the eyes which allowed them to submerge the rest of their head while stalking prey. Their backs were well-supplied with bony plates, as protection against predators. The **aetosaurs** were even more heavily armoured; in fact, they were the reptilian version of the armadillo. They occupied terrestrial habitats, and had a peculiar, almost pig-like snout which they may have used to grub for larvae and other invertebrates.

The most formidable archosaurs were the **rauisuchids**. These hulking quadrupeds could achieve an upright stance. Rauisuchids (though not dinosaurs themselves) had massive heads similar in shape to those of the famous meat-eating dinosaurs of later times. Rauisuchid teeth from Fundy are 6 cm (2.3 inches) in length—fully half the size of those from the most famous predator of all time, *Tyrannosaurus rex*. Undoubtedly, rauisuchids were the tyrants of the Late Triassic.

Despite their formidable nature, rauisuchids, and along with them, phytosaurs and aetosaurs, all disappeared by the end of the Triassic.

Three other branches of the archosaurian tree, however, grew in strength during the Late Triassic to flourish in the Jurassic. One was the crocodilians. You would hardly recognize these ancient crocodiles as such today. They could rear up on their strong hind legs and sprint, using their long tail to balance body and head. Also, they were terrestrial in lifestyle. Another was the flying reptiles, the pterosaurs, and the last, of course, was the dinosaurs.

Looking back over the Triassic, we see that the Early Triassic was dominated by mammal-like reptiles (dicyno-donts and cynodonts); the Middle Triassic by various kinds of archosaurs; but, by the Late Triassic, the Age of Dinosaurs had already dawned. This final transition is evident in Fundy where numerous dinosaur footprints begin to appear in the Late Triassic sediments.

Archosaurs:
Ravisuchid attacking
an Aetosaur

FIRST DINOSAURS

This brings us to the question, what is a dinosaur anyway? In 1841, Sir Richard Owen coined the name dinosaur, meaning "terrible lizard," for a group of large extinct animals (some dinosaurs, some not). It has proven a durable term that vividly conjures up images of the great predatory dinosaurs, such as *Tyrannosaurus rex*.

However, dinosaurs came in all shapes and sizes, from the 80-tonne, plant-eating sauropods of the Late Jurassic to the robin-sized carnivore that left its tracks in the Fundy muds, as the Age of Dinosaurs was just dawning.

They share with other archosaurs certain characteristics, such as two "windows" in the skull behind the eye. In addition, all archosaurs had an opening in front of the eye, the *antorbital fenestra*, which may have contained a gland for excreting salt, a problem in the arid environments that fostered dinosaurs. Also, in common with other archosaurs, the dinosaur's front limbs were usually smaller and more lightly built than the hind limbs.

A: Saurischian, or "lizard-hipped," dinosaur

B: Ornithischian, or "bird-hipped," dinosaur

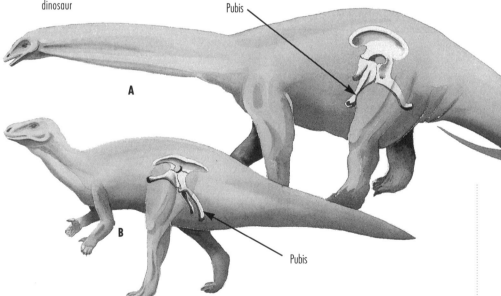

A

Pubis

B

Pubis

Was there any characteristic that distinguished the dinosaurs from their archosaurian cousins? The answer is, "Yes, a fully upright gait." This final refinement in posture set the dinosaurs apart from all other reptiles. The earliest dinosaurs were bipedal, that is, they walked on their hind legs the same as humans. The erect posture gave the dinosaurs distinct advantages: they could run with greater ease and therefore longer, useful when either pursuing prey or fleeing predators. This agility may have given them a competitive edge over other archosaurs (though it is difficult to imagine the early dinosaurs outcompeting the rauisuchids.) Others say that dinosaurs were no better adapted and merely got a lucky break (*see Chapter* 6).

The bipedal locomotion was the result of certain skeletal changes. The limbs supported the body from beneath, as in mammals, rather than from the sides as in early reptiles, which were sprawlers. Later archosaurs, like rauisuchids, had assumed a semi-erect posture in which a headless femur fit into the hip socket like a column. In dinosaurs, however, the femur had a bulb, or head, on the end that fit into the socket at a right angle, allowing the leg to swing freely. The result was a bipedal creature that balanced remarkably on its toes.

The oldest dinosaur dates from the Late Triassic, 230–225 mya. It was found in the Ishigulasto badlands of northwest Argentina by Paul Soreno of the University of Chicago. He named this dog-sized carnivore *Eoraptor*, or "dawn plunderer."

The dinosaurs that followed fell into two groups. Dinosaurs with a pelvis resembling modern lizards, that is, pointing down and forward, were called **saurischian**, or "lizard-hipped,"

Posture and gait in the archosaurs:
A: Sprawling gait (primitive archosaur)
B: Semi-erect gait (rauisuchid)
C: Fully-upright gait (dinosaur)

dinosaurs. Those with a pelvis that was birdlike—with the pubis pointing back as in birds—were called **ornithischian**, or "bird-hipped," dinosaurs.

Two main branches of lizard-hipped dinosaurs developed: two-legged, flesh-eating **theropods** ("beast feet"), and four-legged, plant-eating **sauropodomorphs** ("lizard feet"). The latter included the giants of the Late Jurassic, such as ***Brontosaurus***. The earliest type of this large-bodied, big-footed, long-necked dinosaur with a small head were the prosauropods ("before lizard feet"). They arose in the Middle Triassic but survived only into the Early Jurassic.

Atreipus: an early ornithischian dinosaur

The Fundy dinosaurs are easily the oldest in Canada, and those dating from the Triassic are among the oldest known anywhere. The earliest ornithischian dinosaur on record—225 mya—is ***Pisanosaurus***, a bipedal plant-eater, 1 metre (3.2 feet) long, from the Middle Triassic of Argentina. Donald Baird, formerly of Princeton University, collected, at Burntcoat Head, an upper jaw 1.25 cm (0.5 inch)

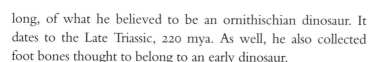

long, of what he believed to be an ornithischian dinosaur. It dates to the Late Triassic, 220 mya. As well, he also collected foot bones thought to belong to an early dinosaur.

The first definite evidence of dinosaurs in Fundy are footprints. A small ornithischian dinosaur (***Atreipus***) left numerous tracks at Paddy's Island, near Wolfville, 220 mya, at the very dawn of the dinosaurs. Also, there are numerous three-toed, bird-like tracks made by a carnivorous dinosaur—a theropod. The trackmaker might well have been ***Coelophysis***.

This predator of the Late Triassic measured a maximum of 2 metres (6.5 feet) to the tip of its long, slender tail, though its body was only slightly larger than a turkey. Unlike any contemporary predator, it lived in relatively large herds. It possessed the unmistakable equipment of an efficient predator: large head and eyes, jaws filled with dozens of knife-sharp teeth, and strong hind legs for leaping. Though primarily a fish eater, it also preyed on other small dinosaurs, reptiles, and even insects.

These first dinosaurs—modest as they were—served warning of the mighty descendants that were to follow in the Age of Dinosaurs.

CHAPTER THREE

SANDSTONE MENAGERIE

Strange, indeed, is this menagerie of remote sandstone days; and the privilege of gazing upon it, and bringing into view one lost form after another, has been an ample recompense for my efforts."

EDWARD HITCHCOCK, 1838

he conventional wisdom has always been, to turn a phrase, "Go West, young paleontologist." And that was what Neil Shubin, now a professor at the University of Pennsylvania, had done. He had followed his graduate advisor at Harvard to the badlands and bonefields of Arizona. There was good reason for those interested in the Age of Dinosaurs to look to the eroded desert landscape. It had already yielded famous caches of fossils. And not only were the fossils abundant, they were well-exposed in the denuded badlands.

On the other hand, the sediments of the Newark Supergroup in Eastern North America were unpromising digging grounds. Though of the same age, they lay under either urban sprawl or vegetation. What fossils they had produced were mostly trackways, not bones. Shubin, however, wanted to work nearer to Harvard, and so, in 1983, he called Olsen, the acknowledged expert on the Triassic-Jurassic boundary. Since his teens, Olsen had been sleuthing the Newark Supergroup basins. He suggested that Shubin look in Fundy, where not only were the rocks of the right age and type but, critically, were well-exposed by the relentless tides. Olsen even suggested that Shubin look closely at Wasson Bluff, where, the year before, he had found scraps of **sphenodontids**, lizard-like creatures.

The first field season appeared to be a total loss. But, back in the laboratory, in Cambridge, Massachusetts, Bill Amaral, Harvard's skilled preparator, plucked from the apparently fossil-barren rock the jaw of a **trithelodont**—an extremely rare mammal-like reptile. It was the first such specimen from North America, and all the incentive Shubin needed for a return visit.

More riches were awaiting him in Fundy's cliffs. The following summer, Shubin and his teammates, Hans-Dieter Sues (now Associate Curator of Vertebrate Paleontology, Royal Ontario Museum) and Paul Olsen, were forced to cautiously work their way along a slippery cliffside above the Bay of Fundy. After some late-night revelry, the men had arrived late for work, and the tides—which wait for no man—had blocked their regular path along the beach. Though the coastline was shrouded in fog, fate would shine on them that day.

Steadying himself as he walked along the loose basalt rubble, Shubin suddenly saw an unusual white speck in the dark lava background. Sues, an expert on Mesozoic reptiles, immediately identified it as the scale from the bony armour of a small crocodilian creature. Suddenly experiencing a strange sensation, Shubin cast a glance around him only to see hundreds of such fossil fragments. "Bones were sticking out all over the place," he would remark later.

For Paul Olsen, this serendipitous discovery was the reward for ten years of diligent searching along the neglected Fundy coastline. Even he was shocked, however, by the richness of the find.

Along with the bones, scutes and skulls of crocodiles were perfectly preserved skulls of lizard-like sphenodontids scattered among the basalt boulders and fisures. Some had perhaps sought shelter there and died; others may have been the remains of a dinosaur's or a crocodile's lunch. Also, there were more rare trithelodont jaws, teeth of small bird-hipped dinosaurs, and abundant fish remains in a layer of greenish rock—all that was left of a shallow lake that once occupied the floor of the ancient rift valley.

Skull of the sphenodontid *Clevosaurus*, a lizard-like reptile

Still other surprises were secreted in the seaside sandstone. In subsequent field seasons, Neil Shubin and Robert Grantham, Geology Curator of the Nova Scotia Museum, found the partial skeleton of a prosauropod protruding from ancient, brick-red sand dune deposits. As well, a specimen of world-class quality—the articulated hindquarters of a baby prosauropod—came to light.

NOVA SCOTIA'S JURASSIC PARK

For the paleontologist, the difficult task of discovering fossils is only the beginning of his or her work. The fossil then must be prepared by carefully removing its matrix of rock with carbide needles and diamond blades. It can take a professional preparator hundreds of hours of painstaking work to prepare a single fossil for examination. Even then, the scientist is presented with only scant evidence—isolated bones, or a partial skeleton, or a few footprints—from which to identify and reconstruct a long-extinct animal. Although there are some extremely well-preserved specimens, such as the sphenodontid skulls and prosauropod skeletons, many of the Fundy fossils are pieces the size of a matchstick, or smaller. By comparing the specimen with other, perhaps more complete, remains described elsewhere, identification often can be made. A detailed description of the bone fragments can yield a surprising amount of information on the shape, size, and type of animal. Slowly, a picture of the animal emerges out of the mists of time. This process of reconstruction is today's scientific equivalent of the science fiction exercise of cloning a dinosaur as described in the novel and movie *Jurassic Park*.

If, rather than bringing the dinosaurs into the present, you could return to Jurassic time in Nova Scotia, you might well recognize features of the landscape, such as the Cobequids, as they are today. But the land would be populated by a strange cast of reptiles.

Sphenodontids—small, sturdily built reptiles—were the most common animals at Wasson Bluff, indicating that they were the prey animals in this Jurassic ecosystem. Also, their beak-like mouth suggests that they were plant-eaters, which put them near the bottom of the food chain. Sphenodontids are closely related to the tuatara, a relative of lizards, that survives today only on a few small islands off the coast of New Zealand.

In Jurassic times, during the heat of the desert day, some of the cold-blooded sphenodontids may have sought shelter in the shade of the volcanic boulders. It would also have been a good hiding place from the speedy predators which crisscrossed the nearby sand flats in search of food.

Today's traveller would not likely identify these graceful, slim animals as primitive crocodiles. They differed significantly from their modern-day counterparts, both in anatomy and lifestyle. Their long, slender limbs superbly adapted them to hunting on land rather than in water. At 1 metre (3 feet), ***Sphenosuchus*** was small compared to modern crocodiles. Like all archosaurs, it had longer hind than front limbs. Long limbs, a sleek body and slender, whip-like tail combined to make it a fleet-footed predator, so much so that Olsen has called it "the cheetah of its time."

Protosuchus ("first crocodile"), though only 0.3 to 0.5 metres (1 to 1.5 feet) long, was well-equipped for its meat-eating livelihood. It was a sabre-toothed crocodile, sporting two greatly enlarged, serrated teeth on its lower jaw. These weapons fit into notches on either side of the snout, which in these early crocodiles was relatively short and narrow.

Both of these primitive crocodiles preyed upon the smaller sphenodontids and, likely, on each other as well as smaller dinosaurs. They were themselves armoured against attack, having scutes both on their bellies and backs.

Trithelodonts, very advanced mammal-like reptiles, were part of the Jurassic fauna at Parrsboro but you might not have seen them—at least not often. Early mammals and their relatives were nocturnal creatures, coming out only at night in order to avoid predation by the dinosaurs and crocodilians—both daytime prowlers. No doubt they subsisted on insects, which required them to be sensitive and agile. We don't know, however, whether trithelodonts had fur or were covered in reptilian scales, as soft parts of the anatomy have not been preserved. It is quite likely that from the outside they looked very much like modern mammals. Though the Parrsboro fossils indicate an animal the size of a large mouse, trithelodonts could grow as large as Siamese cats.

The world's largest cache of trithelodont remains was unearthed at Parrsboro. Their mammal-like characteristics are apparent in the teeth and jaw. Mammals have specialized canine and incisor teeth for dealing with a variety of food. As well, there are more subtle characteristics that distinguish mammals from reptiles, such as the type of enamel and cusp patterns. Most important, perhaps, is the arrangement of teeth in the jaw. The cheek teeth, pre-molars and molars meet face to face in mammals, making it possible for us to chew our food, something no other animal group can

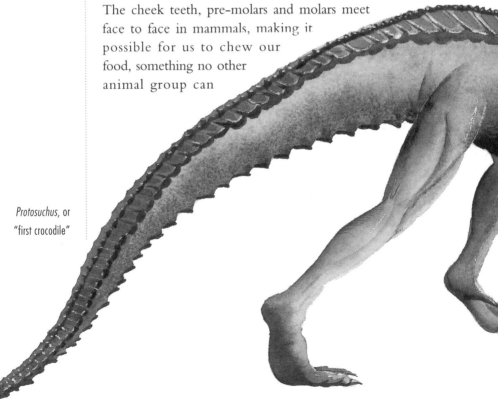

Protosuchus, or "first crocodile"

do. The overall structure of the skull in trithelodonts was very mammal-like. Further study of the very well-preserved teeth and skulls of the Parrsboro trithelodonts may provide new insights into how mammal-like reptiles evolved into true mammals.

Trithelodonts are the animal group most closely related to mammals. They first appear in the fossil record of the Late Triassic. By the Early Jurassic, when the Parrsboro deposits were made, there were already true mammals in other parts of the world. So, by then, trithelodonts were something of living fossils. They may very well have shared Jurassic Nova Scotia with early mammals, which were very modest animals resembling shrews.

Herds of prosauropods plodded across the Fundy stage in Jurassic times. Prosauropods were among the more common dinosaurs of the Late Triassic and Early Jurassic. They appear to have been the first dinosaurs—indeed the first archosaurs—to exploit plant food. In an evolutionary sense, they paved the way for the ascendancy of the giant sauropods of the late Jurassic—the largest land creatures of all time, reaching lengths of 22.5 metres (70 feet) and weights of 78 tonnes.

The adult Parrsboro prosauropod discovered by Grantham and Shubin was a more modest size—2.5 metres (7.5 feet) long and probably weighing less than a man. As the skull was missing it is impossible to definitively identify this animal. A strong candidate is *Ammosaurus*, or sand reptile, known from Arizona and the Connecticut Valley. Or it may have been *Anchisaurus*, the first type of dinosaur discovered in North America. (When first unearthed, in 1818, in the Connecticut Valley, its skeleton was thought to be that of a man.) Or it could have been

Massopondylus, meaning "massive vertebra," named by Sir Richard Owen himself. Until the elusive skull turns up it will not be possible to solve this identity riddle.

All three animals were lightly built dinosaurs with small heads and long necks and tails. Although some argue that they were exclusively bipedal, it is likely that at times they tipped forward to walk on all fours. As well, there is an argument over what prosauropds ate: whether they ate meat (carnivores), plants (herbivores), or both plant and animal matter (omnivores). If they ate meat they probably scavenged dead carcasses; however, the paleontologists generally agree that they were plant-eaters.

Their ability to rear up on their hind legs and their elongated necks allowed them to browse foliage beyond the reach of most other herbivores. Their disappearance in the Early Jurassic may have resulted from the larger sauropod dinosaurs taking over that ecological niche.

Large in the hind quarters, prosauropods had relatively short and slim front limbs, with very distinctive "hands." Hand seems an appropriate term because the fifth finger displayed a long curved claw resembling a thumb. We can only speculate as to the specialized function of this curious digit. The claw might have been a tool for rooting and directing branches to the mouth, or it might have been turned into a formidable weapon, or been used as a grooming tool. Prosauropod teeth were not ideally shaped for

Plant-eating Prosauropod, a saurischian dinosaur

chewing. But stones called **gastroliths**—polished smooth by digestive acids and the friction of rubbing against one another—have been found in their stomachs. They used gastroliths to grind food in the same way as birds employ stones in their gizzards.

Fundy is one of the very few places in the world where stomach stones have been found in context. In the late 1980s, Grantham and Shubin uncovered a prosauropod skeleton with small, polished stomach stones under the ribcage.

What was interesting about the stones themselves was that they were not basalt, but polished cobbles of metamorphic rocks from the Cobequids. These stones told a story.

The prosauropod obviously had been to the Highlands, miles from the rift valley, to pick up the stomach stones. Stones were not the only things inside the prosauropod's gut. In addition there was a jaw of a sphenodontid. The fact that there was only a jaw probably means that it had scavenged it not for the flesh but for the calcium, such as contemporary animals frequently do.

There was more to the story. The skeleton was found directly under a talus slope deposit—a rockfall of basalt. Olsen doesn't know whether the animal was buried by the rockfall after death, or whether it was fatally crushed. Either may have happened.

Bones, when analysed in context with their environment, not only tell us something about the animal's appearance but its lifestyle as well—and, in rare instances, can even reveal details of its death.

Like all reptiles, dinosaurs lost and replaced teeth throughout their lifetime. Teeth are not only among the most common body fossils but are among the most useful, for they tell us what animals ate. From teeth and bones found at Wasson Bluff, we know that there were other plant-eating dinosaurs, besides prosauropods, in Nova Scotia. They may have been **fabrosaurs**, small, 1 meter (3.2 feet) long, bipedal ornithischians which, some say, were the ancestors of all other bird-hipped dinosaurs. They were usually lightly built with hollow bones, long tails, long legs, and a four-toed foot. Fabrosaurs appeared in late Triassic times and survived for another 55 million years.

The Parrsboro animal was likely *Lesothosaurus*, originally identified from the Lesotho region of South Africa. This was a lightly built animal with long hind limbs and tail, all of which made it a fast runner. Its front limbs had five fingers, not unlike our own hands, but sporting claws. Its teeth were distinctively shaped like little arrowheads, which it used for slicing through tough plant food.

There were also meat-eating theropod dinosaurs roaming Parrsboro's environs on the look-out for a meal. Among them were the **coelurosaurs**, or "hollow-tailed reptiles." These were slender, fast-running predators with long necks, small heads well-supplied with teeth serrated as steak knives, and long arms which ended in taloned grasping hands.

Teeth found in Fundy probably belonged to *Syntarsus*, an agile predator that could reach lengths of 3 metres (10 feet), but more commonly was half that size. It lived along streams, often in herds, and ate other small dinosaurs,

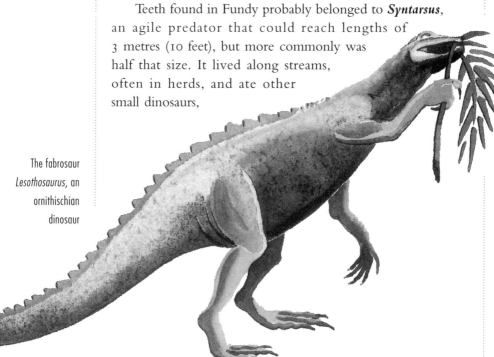

The fabrosaur *Lesothosaurus*, an ornithischian dinosaur

reptiles and fish. It strongly resembled *Coelophysis*—a 1.8 meter (6 foot) long, late Triassic predator—though *Syntarsus* had a larger head and jaw, and, in general, was more powerfully built. In that sense, it anticipated the larger predators, such as *Allosaurus*, the most powerful and deadly dinosaur of the Late Jurassic. *Syntarsus* had sturdy hind legs and a fused ankle, or tarsus, thus its name meaning "fused tarsus." These features gave it greater speed and endurance in running. It may have hopped like a kangaroo, an unpredictable mode of locomotion that would have aided it in escaping predators.

The question then becomes, what was *Syntarsus* trying to escape? No bones of large meat-eating dinosaurs—the so-called **carnosaurs**—have been found yet in Fundy. However, there are tracks made by animals much larger than any indicated by skeletal remains. The tracks were likely made by the carnivorous dinosaur **Dilophosaurus**.

It was 6 metres (20 feet) long, with heavily built hind legs for running, short, relatively feeble forelimbs, and a heavily built head supported on a stout, sturdy neck. The distinguishing feature of *Dilophosaurus* ("two-crested reptile") was the two ridges of thin bone that formed showy crests atop its snout. Paleontologists speculate that they functioned as a display mechanism to claim territory or food, or possibly to attract mates.

The theropod *Syntarsus*, a meat-eating saurischian dinosaur

Dilophosaurus' jaws were relatively weak compared to later "carnosaurs," as was its neck, leading some to believe that it was a scavenger. It could have effectively subdued prey, however, by slashing and tearing with its long, slender front teeth. It may well have preyed upon the large prosauropods as well as the fabrosaurs and coelurosaurs. *Dilophosaurus* has been called "the terror of the Early Jurassic"—and perhaps is the best reason for not wanting to return to Jurassic Nova Scotia.

The large meat-eating dinosaur *Dilophosaurus*

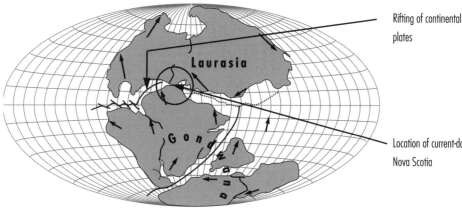

Rifting of continental
plates

Location of current-day
Nova Scotia

JURASSIC'S ONE EARTH

The supercontinent Pangaea began to split apart during the Jurassic Period. Massive volcanism that created the North Mountain accompanied this rifting process, which eventually led to the opening of the Atlantic Ocean.

Even though the continental plates had begun to pull apart, the Parrsboro fossils indicate that, in earliest Jurassic times, the land masses remained connected. For example, the sphenodontid specimens at Parrsboro are identical to *Clevosaurus*, a fossil sphenodontid discovered in England in the late 1930s. This similarity suggests that, 200 million years ago, the Atlantic Ocean had not yet opened sufficiently to isolate the two populations.

Also, *Protosuchus* from Fundy is identical to specimens from China and South America, which strongly suggests that the continents formed a single land mass during the Late Triassic and Early Jurassic Periods.

Similarly, trithelodonts from Fundy are identical to those from the Stromberg Formation of South Africa. This, too, reflects the geography of the Jurassic. Nova Scotia was then nestled against North Africa, in the area of Morocco. Therefore, trithelodonts from Nova Scotia and South Africa, though separated by 5 000 kilometres (3 000 miles), were then residents of a continuous landmass, and they could have walked from one part of it to another.

Pangaea—"One Earth"—showing the location of Nova Scotia in the Jurassic Period. Rifting between North Africa and the eastern coast of North America led to the opening up of the Atlantic Ocean and the eventual break-up of Pangaea.

CHAPTER FOUR

ON THE FOSSIL TRAIL

*It has often happened to geologists, as to other explorers
of new regions, that footprints in the sand have guided them
to the inhabitants of unknown lands.*
—SIR WILLIAM DAWSON, 1863

pril 10, 1984, was a typically cold, windy Maritime spring day. Parrsboro rock specialist Eldon George was on his four-wheel, all-terrain vehicle cruising the shoreline of the Minas Basin near his Parrsboro home. George was following a passion for rocks and minerals which he had acquired as a boy growing up along these shores, long recognized as a storehouse of geological treasures.

When nine, Eldon had fallen from a barn rafter and splintered his right arm. Poor healing had left him permanently disabled. Unable to swing a baseball bat, he could wield a geologist's hammer. He turned his energy to collecting and preparing the rocks and minerals to be found on the beaches and along seaside cliffs surrounding his home. As an adult, he extended his collecting skills to fossils. He had been credited with a number of important finds, including 300-million-year-old amphibian footprints and remains of a rare lobe-finned fish. His prowess as a finder of fossils was about to increase.

As he stooped over the "buggy" to warm his hands, inconspicuous imprints in the red sandstone caught his expert eye. " My God, those look like tracks," he said to himself. He scraped away some loose sand with his hand, then worked feverishly with his jacknife. Another then another track revealed itself.

The 16-by-14 inch (40 cm by 35 cm) slab of pale red sandstone was crisscrossed by five tiny trackways, as if the creature had been practising a dance step. The three-toed footprints identified it as belonging to a theropod dinosaur.

Digits, footpads and claw marks were clearly visible. What was most remarkable was the footprint's size—no bigger than a penny. They were, as it turned out, the smallest dinosaur footprints ever uncovered.

THE SCIENCE OF TRACKWAYS

"There is no branch of detective science which is so important and so much neglected as the art of tracing footsteps," wrote Conan Doyle, the creator of Sherlock Holmes, in 1891. His statement might well be applied to the science of fossil trackways and traces.

The study of trackways is called *ichnology* (from the Greek *ikhnos*, track). Strong interest attended the discovery of trackways in England and New England, in the early 19th century. The first evidence of dinosaurs were three-toed, theropod footprints uncovered by a student named Pliny

MAKING TRACKS

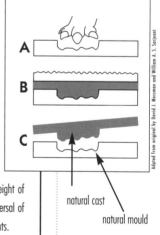

natural cast

natural mould

Adapted from original by David J. Mossman and William A. S. Sarjeant

In order for a dinosaur to leave its track, conditions had to be ideal, both before and after it passed by. The ground had to be soft. Usually it was a muddy surface as you might find along a lakeshore or stream.

The weight of the animal impressed the footprint into the muddy ground (**A**). The sun then baked the footprint until it dried out and became hard. Strong seasonal rains washed sand from the Cobequid highlands into the rift valley, filling the tracks with coarse sediment (**B**). The difference in consistency between the two layers was important in preserving the trackway.

Eventually, the trackway was covered by many layers of sand and mud. The weight of this material turned the mud and sand into stone over many millions of years. In a reversal of the process, erosion by water and wind—and, in Fundy, the tides—exposed the footprints.

All the dinosaur footprints found in Fundy so far have been natural casts, that is, the raised sandy material that originally filled in the footprint. (The sunken part, when visible, is called a natural mould.) The cast becomes apparent when the two layers of stone—the mudstone and sandstone—split apart (**C**).

Moody, in 1802, when he was plowing his father's field in South Hadley, Massachusetts. In keeping with the accepted view of Earth history at that time, the tracks were thought to have been made by "Noah's raven."

Subsequently, many dinosaur trackways came to light in the New England quarries which supplied brownstone for Manhattan's mansions. Edward B. Hitchcock, the president of Amherst College, spent a lifetime collecting and writing about the Connecticut Valley trackways. He died in 1865, persisting in his view that the tracks were made by birds: "Now I have seen, in scientific vision, a [wingless] bird, some twelve or fifteen feet high,—nay, large flocks of them,—walking over the muddy surface, followed by many others of analogous character, but of smaller size."

Tracks are much more abundant than bony remains and, in many cases, extinct animals are known only from trackways.

However, the spectacular bone discoveries of the late 19th and early 20th centuries in western North America diverted interest from the study of trackways. In recent years, ichnology has been undergoing a revival.

CARBONIFEROUS TRACKWAYS

The Fundy region has long had a reputation for yielding scientifically important trackways.

In 1841, Sir William Logan, first director of the Geological Survey of Canada, was intrigued by some building stone on the wharf at Windsor, Nova Scotia. His inquiry about its origins lead him to Horton Bluff, overlooking the Avon estuary, where he discovered a set of seven footprints made by an amphibian some 350 million years before. It was a radical discovery for, until then, it was believed that fishes were the only vertebrates and that they did not crawl onto land until the Permian Period, some 50 million years later. Logan's was the first evidence of life's first tentative steps onto land.

However, when he displayed the tracks to a meeting of the prestigious Geological Society of London, his colleagues, including Sir Richard Owen, failed to acknowledge the importance of his find, holding to the old belief that fishes were the only vertebrates in the Coal Age. It was left to Sir William Dawson to vindicate his friend's discovery in his classic book, *Air Breathers of the Coal Period*.

Dawson himself subsequently found prints of both amphibians and reptiles at Joggins, Horton, and Windsor. He speculated that these "air breathers of the coal period ... haunted tidal flats and muddy shores, perhaps emerging from the water that they might bask in the sun, or possibly searching for food." The probable trackmakers were *Dendrerpeton* and *Hylonomus*, among others.

Trackways resembling the tread marks of a caterpillar tractor often crisscross sandstone slabs at Joggins. These were made by the era's largest land animal, *Arthropleura*, which attained lengths of 2 metres (6.5 feet) and resembled a giant sowbug. Another invertebrate, the horseshoe crab, left its much smaller—2.5 cm (1 inch) across—trackways in Coal Age sediments. They make a kind of herringbone pattern, with the tail drag forming a center line.

In 1908 the National Museum of Canada erected impressive scaffolding at East Bay, near Parrsboro, in order to salvage from the vertical cliff face a particularly striking set of amphibian footprints.

For the rest of the 20th century, until the early 1960s, the Fundy fossil trail was conspicuously cool. Then, in 1964, two students conducting a hydrological survey stumbled upon some very large fossil tracks, 50 metres (165 feet) offshore from Horton Bluff. They were exposed at extreme low tide, when a storm had swept clean the overlying mud.

The discoverer, Dr. David Mossman, now a professor of Geology at Mt. Allison University, in Sackville, N.B., eventually mapped 27 footprints spanning a 20-metre (65-foot) distance. Their preservation in 350-million-year-old sediments made them, at the time, the oldest vertebrate tracks in the fossil record. (They remain the oldest vertebrate fossil trackways ever found in Canada.) Not only were they old, they were of unprecedented size: spaced 0.3 metres (1 foot) apart, each footprint was 0.3 metre (1 foot) long. The tracks are deep with raised edges, suggesting that the animal was heavy and the mud very soft when it waddled by 350 million

Eryops, an amphibian from the Carboniferous period

years ago. The absence of claws and the width of the trackway show it as having been made by an amphibian. It is impossible to identify the animal, as no bones of an amphibian large enough to have made these tracks have ever been found. We can only speculate as to its identity. One candidate is a **labyrinthodont** amphibian related to the semiaquatic predator ***Eryops***.

Eryops was a bulky amphibian that attained lengths of 2 metres (6 feet), and more. Its size and 0.3 meter (1 foot) wide jaws made it a formidable predator in water. On land, however, it lumbered along on short legs and was itself vulnerable to predation.

Donald Baird, formerly of Princeton University, is one of the world's leading ichnologists—experts in the study of fossil tracks. He spent many years investigating the area around Horton Bluff, which he calls "one of the classic fossil localities in the Western Hemisphere." Baird believes the Horton Bluff trackmaker may have been an **embolomere**, an order of extinct amphibians more related to crocodiles than to living frogs or salamanders. If so, it probably had fangs and was the most feared carnivore in the Carboniferous swamp.

In order to save the trackway from ongoing erosion, several years ago the Nova Scotia Museum made plaster casts for future display and study.

TRIASSIC-JURASSIC TRACKWAYS

As the Carboniferous trackways are dominated by amphibians and small reptiles, the Triassic-Jurassic trackways are dominated by dinosaurs and crocodilians. Trackways, therefore, serve as valuable clues to the march of evolution.

It is possible to distinguish the major groups of dinosaurs based on characteristic foot shapes, and, frequently, to distinguish dinosaurs from crocodilians. It is difficult, if not impossible, to identify exactly what animal made a particular trackway. For this reason, trackways are given their own names. Animals known by their footprints are called **ichnofauna**.

Footprints have been uncovered in many areas around the Minas Basin shoreline. McKay Head, east of Wasson Bluff, has been a productive area for footprints. These are some of the footprints that you might come across as you walk along the Fundy shoreline.

DISTINGUISHING AMPHIBIAN AND REPTILE TRACKS

Amphibian trackways are broad and marked by a short stride, indicating the inefficient locomotion of these creatures on land. The trackways of reptiles generally are narrower and the stride longer than in the case of amphibian trackways, indicating more efficient locomotion.

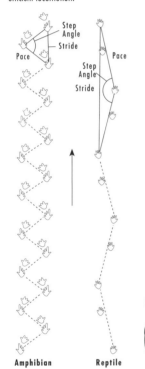

Amphibian   Reptile

Adapted from original by David J. Mossman and William A. S. Sarjeant

Atreipus left both footprints and handprints in Triassic sediments on Paddy Island, near Wolfville, N.S., some 220 mya. This makes it only slightly younger than the famous Ischigualasto fauna of Argentina, home to the world's oldest dinosaur fossils. It appears to have been a small ornithischian dinosaur that often put down its hands.

Coelurosarichnus's palm-size print features a very long sickle-shaped claw on digit two, very similar to that of **Deinonychus**, or "terrible claw," of Early Cretaceous time. It was probably a dinosaur and, if so, was a very odd one for its time. It demonstrates, says Olsen, that there were some very "nasty beasties" around in early dinosaur days.

Batrachopus made trackways from 2 to 6 cm (0.7 to 2.3 inches) in length and displayed five digits on both the hand and foot, of which at least four always appear in the track. As reconstructed from the trackways, the bones of the hand and foot of *Batrachopus* are identical to those of crocodilians.

Batrachopus track, probably a crocodilian like *Protosuchus*

Furthermore, modern crocodiles have the same strongly out-turned, five-fingered hand. All of these lines of evidence point to it being a crocodilian of some sort. Olsen believes that it was almost certainly the long-legged *Protosuchus* whose bones were found at Wasson Bluff.

Otozoum track (hand print), probably a prosauropod

The Fundy Basin has been particularly productive of *Otozoum* prints. More have been uncovered here in the last decade than in the 150 previous years in the Connecticut Valley. These are the largest trackways yet found in the area, measuring up to 50 cm (20 inches) in length and 35 cm (15 inches) in width. The trackmaker remains a mystery. It has been hotly debated whether *Otozoum* was a prosauropod dinosaur or primitive crocodile. Olsen once favoured the crocodile theory, but now agrees with the interpretation of Richard Swann Lull, author of the classic *Triassic Life of the Connecticut Valley*, that *Otozoum* was a prosauropod dinosaur.

A modern seagull might have made the three-toed track we call **Grallator**, it is so bird-like. The three toes are the signature of a theropod dinosaur—a carnivore. This small trackmaker seems to have left its prints the globe over. They were very common in the Connecticut Valley, and the same is true in Fundy. *Coelophysis* probably made the Fundy *Grallator* tracks. *Grallator* prints might also belong to *Syntarsus*, which some feel is merely the Jurassic form of *Coelophysis*.

Grallator track, a small theropod dinosaur

Eubrontes, Connecticut's State fossil, is a large theropod track. As already discussed, one very likely candidate is *Dilophosaurus*. Olsen thinks that *Eubrontes* may simply be an adult version of *Grallator*.

A small, bipedal ornithischian dinosaur, which occasionally put its hands down, was the likely maker of **Anomoepus** tracks. The fabrosaurs are the likely trackmakers.

Eubrontes track, a large theropod dinosaur

Anomoepus track, possibly a fabrosaur

WHAT TRACKWAYS TELL US:

Trackways reveal information about the lives and environment of ancient animals that are not obvious from skeletal remains. Tracks are indisputable evidence of the posture and locomotion of the trackmaker—how they stood, walked, ran, or even swam. For example, trackways offer proof that dinosaurs indeed did stand and walk erect. Bipedal dinosaurs put their feet one in front of another, in a manner very similar to the way that humans walk. The rare occurrence of tail drags suggests that they kept their tail elevated, probably using it as a balancing device.

Most important, trackways offer unique insights into the behaviour of extinct animals. The study of trackways first confirmed that large sauropods were not limited to an aquatic life but were efficient walkers on land—in fact, the largest creatures ever to tread the planet. As well, trackways from State Dinosaur Park at Rocky Hill, Connecticut, suggest that the large predatory species *Eubrontes* could swim in shallow water, using its legs to kick off the bottom and propel itself forward.

The frequency of tracks can serve as a census of the community and offer a glimpse of the ecosystem, for example, predator-prey relationships. In one instance, there are trackways from Texas of a bipedal, carnivorous dinosaur superimposed on *Brontosaurus* trackways, suggesting that the carnivore was stalking the large herbivore.

Trackways have shown that dinosaurs sometimes moved in herds—an advanced social behaviour without close parallel in the reptile world today. They may have done so for defensive purposes. Peace River trackways, in British Columbia, show juvenile footprints of **hadrosaurs** (herbivores of the late Cretaceous) over top of adult ones, indicating the juveniles were trailing behind a frontline of adults. Also, small to medium-sized carnivorous dinosaurs sometimes hunted in packs. *Grallator* and *Eubrontes* tracks from the Connecticut Valley seem to confirm that behaviour. Evidence to date indicates that large carnosaurs, like *Tyrannosaurus rex*, moved singly or, on occasion, in pairs.

Trackways have done much to dispel the long-standing, wrong-headed view that dinosaurs were solitary, plodding, and dim-witted creatures.

A pack of *Coelophysis* leave their tracks (called *Grallator*) in the Jurassic mud

The speed of the animals can be calculated from the pattern and spacing of its footprints. Most footprints are those made by creatures walking. Predatory dinosaurs were brisk walkers, making an average of 5 to 10 kph (between 3 and 6 miles per hour). Footprints of running dinosaurs have also been found occasionally. They indicate that medium-sized carnivores were capable of bursts of speed to 16.5 kph (10 miles per hour). Theropods like *T. rex* may actually have attained speeds twice that fast, up to 40 kph (25 mph). The top speed for herbivores was a much slower 6 kph (4 mph).

It's obvious from the study of trackways that dinosaurs could be very active animals. An increasing number of paleontologists, led by Robert Bakker, author of *The Dinosaur Heresies*, believe that dinosaurs were, in fact, warm-blooded like birds and mammals.

One of the long-standing arguments for dinosaurs having been cold-blooded was their large size. Their small surface area compared to mass would have allowed them to retain heat. However, the small dinosaur that made the trackway found by Eldon George would not have had this advantage; in fact, it would have faced the same problem of heat retention as does a bird of comparable size. Judging from the trackways in Fundy and other basins of the Newark Supergroup, most of the dinosaurs from the Early Jurassic were relatively small, turkey- to ostrich-size. Small size is just another piece of evidence in a still-controversial, but growing, case in favour of the warm-bloodedness of dinosaurs. The most compelling evidence is the many channels found in dinosaur bones. These structures, called Haversian systems, carried rich blood supplies necessary to the metabolism of a warm-blooded animal. Today, they are typical of fast-growing birds and mammals rather than slow-growng, cold-blooded reptiles, such as crocodiles, turtles and lizards.

Trackways also tell us about the environment of the trackmakers. In particular, the depths of tracks are good indicators of the water content of the soils but they can also be used to determine the slope of the ancient landscape, the position of an ancient shoreline, and, in cases where they were made underwater, current direction. Often, trackways occur in mudflats around the margins of lakes. This appears to be the case in the Fundy basin, which was occupied by a seasonal lake. The fluctuating water levels created ideal conditions for the preservation of footprints.

Modern Trackmakers

Many modern tracks and trackmakers are visible on the mudflats bordering the Bay of Fundy—an ideal environment for the short-term preservation of tracks. In late summer when more than one million shorebirds stop over to feed during their annual migration to South America, they leave tiny tracks not unlike those made by the diminutive dinosaurs, 200 million years ago. Sir Charles Lyell first noticed the similarities between the fresh bird tracks in Fundy and the abundant fossil trackways in the Connecticut River valley. In his *Travels in North America*, he wrote: "On the surface of the dried beds of red mud at Wolfville on the Bay of Fundy ... I observed ... the distinct footmarks of birds in regular sequence, faithfully representing in their general appearance the smaller Ornithicnites of high antiquity in the valley of the Connecticut."

Lyell's observations seem to anticipate what now is a widely accepted theory in paleontology that modern birds are the direct descendants of dinosaurs. In fact, birds are nothing less than living dinosaurs. So, it is possible today to see dinosaurs leaving their tracks along the Fundy shore—just as they did 200 million years ago. Perhaps, in the far distant future, someone will find them alongside your own fossilized footprints.

CHAPTER 5

THE LANDSCAPE THEN AND NOW

*Every time I stand before these cliffs, I feel dwarfed
by the immensity of time.*
PAUL OLSEN, 1990

aul Olsen spent six years deciphering the complex geology of Wasson Bluff. "What's funny is a great deal of complication is produced by a very simple cause," he now says. That very simple cause is that the north shore of the Minas Basin parallels—in fact, sits on and was created by—a major fault.

In geology, a fault occurs when the earth's crust is strained past the breaking point and it yields along a crack, or sometimes a series of cracks. This results in the opposing rocks moving in contrary directions—one side rises or sinks relative to its neighbour, or the two sides move laterally, sliding by one another.

The faulting in Fundy occurred during the Triassic-Jurassic periods as the sediments that filled the Fundy basin were being deposited. So, faulting was literally transforming the geology as it was being formed.

The fault is known as a strike-slip fault and is similar to the San Andreas Fault in California, the cause of the San Francisco earthquakes. Fortunately for Nova Scotia, it's no longer a very active fault, and not likely to produce major earthquakes. However, what it has produced is a complicated geological picture which confounded geologists for generations.

In a sedimentary basin such as Fundy, you expect to see a traditional layer-cake geology, that is, one distinct layer of rock laid on top of another, with the youngest rocks on top. In Fundy, however, faulting has chopped the layer cake into many small pieces—and then turned all of them at slightly different angles. The beach cliffs present the viewer with a cross section of this piecemeal, three-dimensional geometry. Walking on the beach is, in a sense, like walking through a maze of these geological chunks, created by the twisting and turning of forces within the earth.

In approximately 5 kilometres (3 miles) of shoreline you will find several paleo-environments: river channels wending their way to a lake; a shallow lake (playa) lapping up against the basalt cliff; wind-blown dune sands; and basalt talus slope tumbling down a fossil cliff. Each of these ancient environments has preserved a record of life.

COLLECTING

All collecting is prohibited by law at the protected Special Place just west of Wasson Bluff. Do not use rock hammers anywhere in these outcrops; these fossils are small, rare and always important to science. Outside the protected site, it is against the law to remove or disturb any fossil in the bedrock. **All fossils in Nova Scotia have this protection.**

If you had been alive 200 million years ago, you could have walked from one environment to another. The contemporary environment in many ways reflects the complexity of the ancient environment. In the space of a few hundred metres, you go from a cliff, to a beach, to the Bay. As you walk along the beach you are tracing the footfalls of dinosaurs which left their trackways on the muddy shores of a lake. In Jurassic times, this shallow lake lapped against the cliff base where, today, the Bay of Fundy tides ebb and flow.

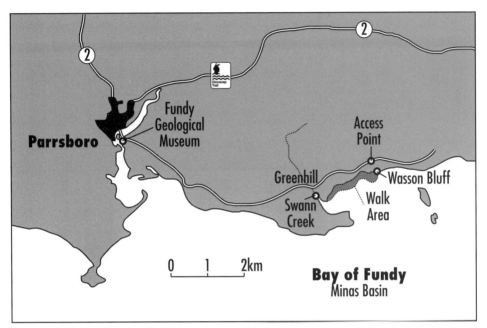

A NOTE OF CAUTION

CONSULT TIDE TABLES OR NEWSPAPERS FOR THE TIDE TIMES.

The tides in the Minas Basin rise 14 m (44 feet). It is best to plan your beach walk when the tide is going out, which will allow you several hours on the shore without fear of becoming stranded by the rapidly rising tide. Fisheries and Oceans Daily Tide Information: 426-5494

This section of the beach is bounded by steep cliffs which are prone to collapse. For your own safety do not climb on the cliffs or stand near or under the cliffs. As an added safety measure wear a hard hat at the base of the cliffs.

To reach Wasson Bluff

To reach Wasson Bluff from the Fundy Geological Museum, turn right onto Riverside Road in the direction of Greenhill. Drive for 8.5 kilometres (5.3 miles) east, continuing past the end of the pavement and crossing Swann Creek. Approximately a kilometer past the creek, an inconspicuous dirt road appears on the right. Pull over, park, and follow the road on foot to the beach. The section begins across Wasson Brook to the west, on your left facing the cliffs. This is Wasson Bluff, the site of the spectacular discovery made by Paul Olsen and Neil Shubin in 1986.

A WALK ALONG THE BEACH:
WASSON BLUFF TO SWANN CREEK

SECTION 1

When you look up into the mouth of Wasson Brook, you see at **A** layers of red, slightly grey to maroon, shale and sandstone beds that were laid down 300 million years ago, in the Pennsylvanian Period. In those rocks we find footprints of ancient amphibians and one of the earliest reptiles. Those layers are standing up on edge, because they were compressed when Africa crushed into North America in the process of assembling the supercontinent of Pangaea.

As you walk to the west along Wasson Bluff, immediately you see a change of character. You see (partially covered by bushes) layers of crumbly greenish-grey and purple sandstones and layers of soft gravel sitting on top of the maroon strata, which are 300 million years old. These soft, gravelly rocks are 202-million-year-old Triassic -

The human figure in these illustrations is used to give a sense of scale to the cliffs.

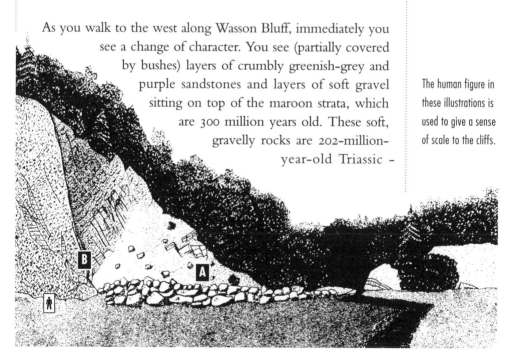

sediments (Blomidon Formation). So, there is a 110-million-year gap between the two sets of layers. (In geology, this is known as an unconformity.) During that time, as Africa crushed into North America, mountains were formed and mountains were eroded. At 210-220 million years ago, Africa and North America began to pull apart again, creating great rift valleys along eastern North America, including the Fundy Basin.

At **B**, sitting on top of this deposit of shales and conglomerates, you will see a lava flow—a greenish grey massive unit, with structures that look like columns. This is called columnar basalt and was formed as the lava cooled.

This basalt flow was vast, extending from Parrsboro all the way to the Gulf of Maine at least as far south as Boston. Cape Blomidon, North Mountain to Brier Island, Cap d'Or, Ile Haute, and Grand Manan Island are all pieces of the giant lava flow. It was more than a flow; in fact, it was a lake that filled the basin. In the shales right underneath that lava flow is the Triassic-Jurassic boundary. This threshold in time marks a major extinction event. More than 45% of all families of creatures living on land, and a similar percentage of creatures living in the oceans, disappear from the fossil record. There are many theories for why this mass extinction occurred but one of the more popular is the asteroid impact theory *(see Chapter 6).*

Columnar basalt

B

Section 2

As you continue walking along the cliff face you are parallelling a fault. In fact, the face of the cliff is one side of the fault. It is very unusual to find such a feature preserved. On the right hand, the basalt cliff has a crushed appearance rather than the clean columnar appearance that it did at **B**. This is what you might expect where a fault has cut into a lava flow. To your left, beginning at **C**, is a layer of orange sandstone at beach level. It has slumped down because of that fault, which is almost vertical. That sandstone (McCoy Brook Formation) is Jurassic in age. In the basalts above, you can find various members of the zeolite family of minerals occupying former gas cavities in the lava flows. Look for: *chabazite* (orange rhombs), *analcite* (milky globular), *heulandite* (pearly coffin shapes) and *stilbite* (whitish sheaves of wheat).

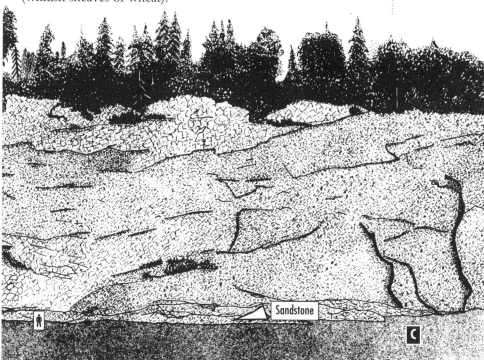

Sandstone

C

SECTION 3

At **D**, the fault forks: one half continues straight west and the other half turns left, at about 45 degrees. Also at **D**, you see the first chunk of fossil basalt talus slope. Just as now you have a cliff of basalt and it crumbles to make a talus slope, the same thing happened in ancient times when there was a cliff. These faults existed in the Jurassic and they formed cliffs of basalt that don't look very different from what you see in place now. Animals liked to live on the rocks and in the spaces between the rocks; their remains, and the scraps of their meals, are preserved in the red and orange sandstones that filled up the spaces between the basalt blocks.

Talus slope

Basalt stack

D

SECTION 4

In Sections 4 and 5 between **E** and **F**, you have very well-preserved basalt talus deposits that accumulated along this cliff in the Jurassic. It's in this area, especially at **E**, that by far the richest accumulations of bone are found. However, the bones are scrappy—partial skulls, legs, and lots of small individual bone pieces. Good skeletons with articulated bones are not found here, for two reasons, according to Paul Olsen: "One, I think we're dealing with the remains of lunches here. (We don't actually have who was having lunch, just the leftovers.) Secondly, these basalt talus slopes move slightly—they creep through time—and the sandstone in them moves too, and that tends to break a lot of the bones."

Talus Slope

E

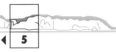

SECTION 5

The most common bones are those of the long-legged protosuchid crocodiles. Second in abundance are trithelodonts (mammal-like reptiles); third sphenodontids, fourth, the very scrappy remains of dinosaurs, including a small ornithischian dinosaur, probably a fabrosaur, and a small theropod dinosaur. Much of the material appeared chewed.

Olsen and Shubin also found **coprolites**—petrified feces, or "dino dung"—suggesting that this was an ancient lunch and rest stop. Who was having lunch? It appears that dinosaurs and crocodiles were feeding on each other. In some instances, animals may have crawled into the spaces and died there.

Talus slope

Section 6

At **F**, the talus slope abruptly ends at a fault, which is coming straight out of the cliff at you. The basalt cliff to your left, in fact, is exactly the same basalt layer as you encountered between **B** and **C**. The confusion is created by the faulting.

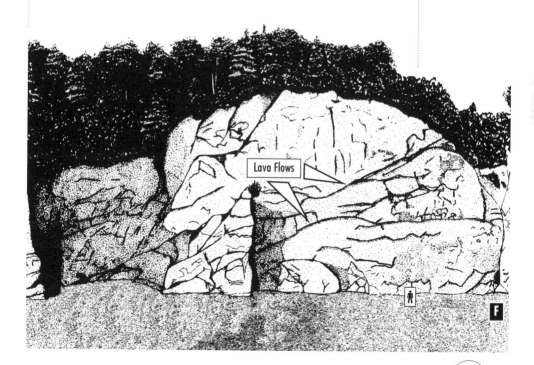

Lava Flows

SECTION 7

As you walk from **F** to **G** you can see a number of reddish layers in the cliff face. Those are the contacts between successive lava flows.

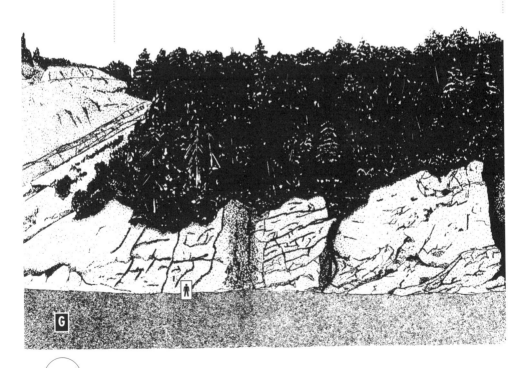

SECTION 8

Then, at **H**, there is another fault coming straight out of the cliff. It is on a diagonal and, in fact, forms the cliff between **H** and **I**. A third of the way between **H** and **I**, you can see, angling 45 degrees to the right, another boundary between two lava flows.

Between **I** and **J**, you see this purple and green layer lapped on top of the basalt flow. This so-called "fish bed" forms a little wedge shape between **I** and **J**. Above that wedge is talus slope. This was not formed by faulting as was seen previously. The lake actually lapped against the basalt cliff, cutting a notch—preserved as a fossilized wave-cut notch—and causing blocks of basalt to fall off the cliff. Wave action has concentrated fish bones in the nooks and crannies of this fossilized little boulder heap. Also, among the fish bones, dinosaur bones were found. This is the first place along your walk where adequate remains of

Talus slope deposit

Fossil cliff

Fish bed

Lava Flow boundary

J I H

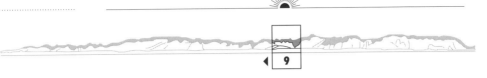
dinosaurs were found—in this case, ornithischian dinosaurs, the plant-eating dinosaur group. Also, there are the teeth of freshwater sharks. They were 0.3 to 0.6 metres (1 to 2 feet) long, about the size of dogfish that now frequent the Bay of Fundy. In addition, there are several kinds of primitive bony fishes with heavy rhombic scales.

Section 9

If you go just a little bit further to the west, at **J**, you see a wall of orange sandstone, running diagonally up to blocks of basalt that look like they fell off the cliff onto the sandstone. These are sandstones formed on the shores of shallow lakes and by rivers and small streams. In this sandstone were found the only articulated remains at Wasson Bluff: a skeleton of a sphenodontid, as well as a skull and the partly articulated skeleton of a baby prosauropod dinosaur. They were buried by

Wind-blown sands

Lake bed

K A J

sand in a stream, or along a shallow lake. These baby sauropod remains rival the famous baby duck-billed dinosaurs found by Jack Horner in Montana.

Several paleoenvironments are preserved in Sections 8 and 9: basalt cliff and talus slope, ancient lakebed, and wind-blown sands that were deposited on top of the dried lakebed. At **K**, in the same layer, is where the second major discovery at Wasson Bluff was made. Olsen first found disarticulated jaws of sphenodontids and scutes of crocodiles. Later, Neil Shubin found the first trithelodont at this spot.

Section 10

From **K** to **L** you see intensely red sandstones. These are fossil dunes deposited by wind. In between some of these layers of dunes, there are basalt blocks that must have rolled down from a nearby cliff, further in the background. These fossil dunes extend from **K** to **N**. Concentration of bones is extremely low here.

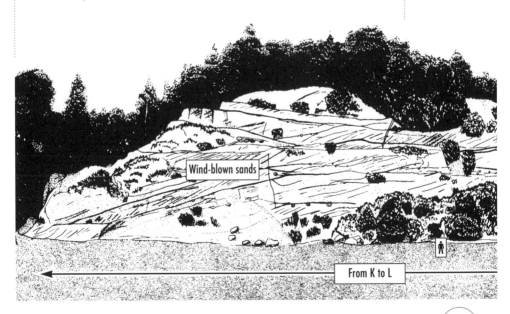

Wind-blown sands

From K to L

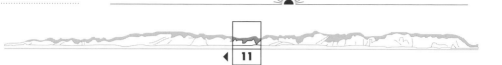

SECTION 11

Near **L**, the skeleton of a prosauropod whose bones seem to have been scattered by ancient scavengers was discovered.

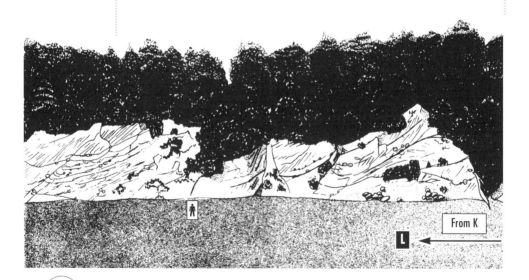

SECTION 12

As you move to **M**, you now can see what the relationship of these dune sands are to the basalts. The vertical face of basalt at M is a fossil cliff of basalt against which dune sands piled up. You can see, in cross section, triangular piles of basalt rubble that have fallen off that cliff and accumulated right next to it. This shows the origin of the other basalt blocks observed between the layers of sand dunes, between **K** and **M**. Boulders just rolled off the cliff and onto the dunes.

To the left, between **M** and **N**, is a big face of basalt. In this zone faults are coming out of the cliffs toward you. These faults cut up the basalt and the dune sands. Directly above **N**, a pile of basalt talus slope buried another prosauropod skeleton. This was the animal in which the rare stomach stones, or gastroliths, were found.

← To N on next page → **M**

SECTION 13

Between **N** and **O** you see a big block of basalt that is bathed in basalt talus. It has fallen off the massive cliff of basalt directly to the left of **O**. At **O**, there is a major fault. This was actually the main fault that resulted in the unique accumulation of sediments and fossils along the entire section seen so far, beginning at Wasson Bluff. The fault formed a pocket on top of the lava flow. If something died in this depression, it didn't wash away but was buried by incoming sediments. In most other places, the animal would have remained exposed on the surface and been scavenged and eroded away. In this pocket, however, it was preserved. In simple terms, it was a hole in the ground created by faulting along the strike-slip fault zone. This pocket was alternately filled by a lake and, when it dried up, by sand dunes. In the process, it also became a rich resting place for fossils. Teeth of small carnivorous dinosaurs are found here.

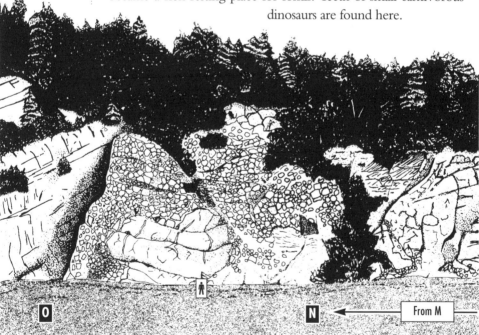

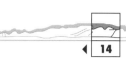
SECTION 14

Different layers of basalt lava are clearly visible between **O** and **P**.

Lava flows

P ◀————————————————————— From O

SECTION 15

From **P** *to* **Q** *is the most dangerous section along the entire walk as indicated by the biggest talus cones on the beach, where basalt rubble has fallen from the cliffs. Fatalities have occurred here from these rockfalls. You should exercise* ***extreme caution***, *keeping well clear of the cliffs.*

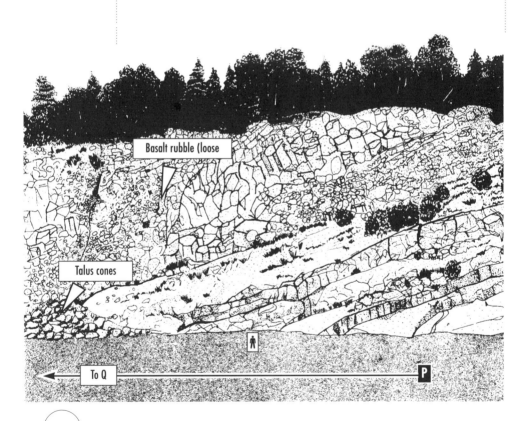

Basalt rubble (loose

Talus cones

To Q

P

SECTION 16

These lava flows occurred during the extrusion of the North Mountain basalt. As the lava cooled it formed clearly visible hexagonal cooling joints, typical of columnar basalt.

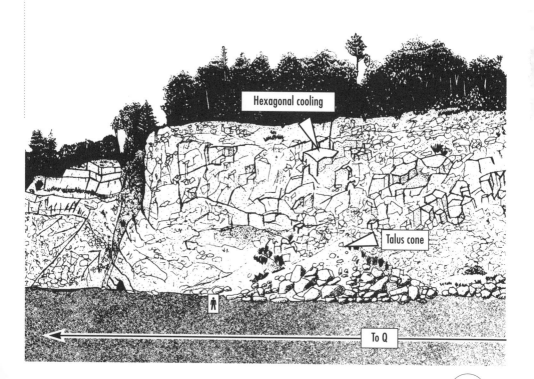

Hexagonal cooling

Talus cone

To Q

SECTION 17

Between **Q** and **R** small faults are visible.

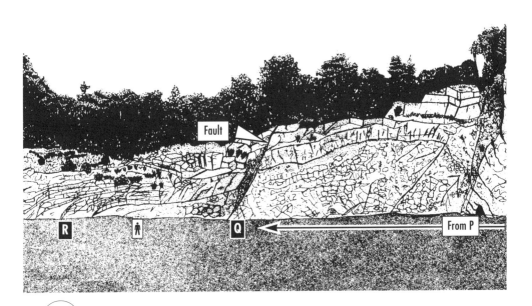

Section 18

At **S**, the basalt appears to be lying on top of the McCoy Brook sedimentary rocks. This is an illusion created by faulting.

Between **S** and **T** you again encounter contact between the McCoy Brook formation and the North Mountain basalt. Note that these once-horizontal lake beds are standing straight up. They gradually become lower in dip, from **T** to **W**. Evidently, after the rift valley formed, there were stretching movements between North America and Africa which locally shoved some of the McCoy Brook formation up into these vertical formations, such as at **T**. Unlike the lake beds encountered earlier, these are very fossil-poor.

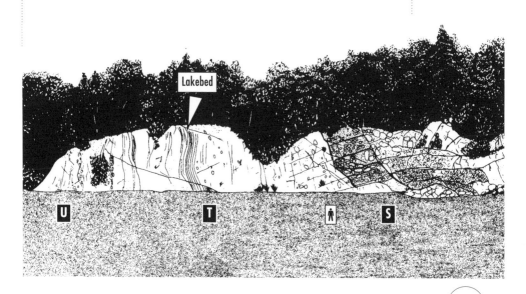

Lakebed

SECTION 19

As you walk from **T** to **U**, the layers become more and more gently dipping—from 45 degrees to only 10 degrees at **Y**. There are very few fossils in this section. The most common fossils are at **V** and **W**, and they are fossil roots, indicating that there was a good development of soils. These were conifers (***Cheirolepids***), which could grow to enormous heights. The ones here were somewhat shrubby. They formed the primary fodder for the prosauropod dinosaurs.

At **W**, you start picking up a different kind of rock again. It looks a little like the talus slope deposits, but these are mud flow deposits of basalt. Such modern-day flows are called **lahars**, which are volcanic deposits that have been mobilized as a mudflow. This kind of lahar was coming off a cliff, in rough topography.

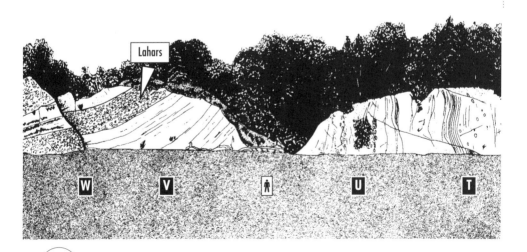

Lahars

W   V   U   T

SECTION 20

There is a fault at **X**. To the left of **Y**, you see more light-coloured McCoy Brook formation. It was deposited in streams and very shallow lakes, and laps up on top of the lahar. This is the end of the distinctive stratigraphy in this area.

THE DAY AFTER

Here we had many bizarre reptile species meandering in the shallow lake, very swift animals living along the shore, and mammal-like species inhabiting the underbrush of the late Triassic forests. Then we come to a barrier in prehistory through which relatively few species passed. Clearly, something sudden and violent had occurred.

PAUL OLSEN, 1990

I t is the twilight of the Triassic Period, more than 200 million years ago. As the sun sets behind distant hills, small, insectivorous reptiles nestle among the underbrush and fallen leaves of a forest of luxurious ferns, dense stands of giant horsetail rushes, and palm-like cycads. One such is a procolophonid. Spikes fringe the back of its skull, making it look like the equivalent of a horned toad. It gulps 1e odd insect which drones close by.

Also hidden in the underfoliage's shadows are mouse-like ancestors of the mammals. They, too, are searching for an insect meal in the leaf litter.

Camouflaged among the dense vegetation fringing a pond is a 4.5-metre (15-foot) long phytosaur, a crocodile-like reptile with a long, narrow snout well-supplied with sharp conical teeth. Bony plates form an effective armour down its back and tail. As formidable a predator as the phytosaur is in its own right, it needs protection from the rauisuchids—the *Tyrannosaurus rexes* of the Triassic.

Skull of a Procolophonid, a reptile

Seemingly passive as a log, the phytosaur waits patiently for an unwary amphibian or reptile to venture within striking distance. Another of its kind lurks offshore, ready to snatch a hapless fish feeding in the shallows. Its nostrils rest on a dome between and in front of its eyes, acting as a kind of snorkel that allow it to lie submerged, motionless, for long periods.

Phytosaur, a crocodile-like archosaur

In the failing light, there are flashes of movement at the forest edge. A pack of 1-metre (3.2-foot) long, lightly-built **coelurasaurs** cautiously approach the waterside in search of a drink. An anxious phytosaur makes a premature lunge, startling the dainty dinosaurs into hasty retreat.

Suddenly, in the distance, the fiery tail of a meteorite blazes its path across the darkening sky. The horizon is illuminated with a flash of apocalyptic light.

This scenario, vividly painted by Hans-Dieter Sues and Paul Olsen, is an attempt to explain the sudden disappearance of nearly half the earth's creatures at the end of the Triassic Period.

According to this so-called asteroid impact theory, the meteorite blasted a hole in the earth's crust, 100 kilometres (60 miles) in diameter, unleashing a calamitous chain of events. A fireball sped halfway across North America, consuming all in its path. Billions of tonnes of dust mushroomed into the atmosphere, darkening the skies for months. Soot from the kindling of massive forest fires further screened vital sunlight.

Photosynthesis was impaired, causing a drastic collapse of the planet's food production system. The effects rippled through the food chain.

Before the biosphere—earth's ecosystem—could begin to stabilize and repair itself, fully half of the earth's creatures had died out. Gone were the phytosaurs, procolophonids, the aetosaurs, large amphibians such as **metoposaurs**, all of the large mammal-like reptiles, and even the seemingly invincible rauisuchids.

These groups of land animals, as well as half of the marine groups, in fact, do disappear from the fossil record, at or near the Triassic-Jurassic (T–J) boundary, 200 million years ago. All traces of these typical Triassic animals—bones and footprints—vanish.

THE GREAT DYINGS: SLOW OR SUDDEN?

The mass extinction at the Triassic-Jurassic boundary was but one of many that have punctuated earth history. There have been as many as 13 "great dyings" in the last 600 million years. In that vast expanse of time, 20 percent of all terrestrial families, 17 percent of all marine families, and 14 percent of all freshwater families have disappeared.

Paleontologists have been struggling to answer the obvious question—Why? Essentially, theorists fall into one of two camps: the gradualists or the catastrophists. The former say that species went extinct over relatively long periods of time due to a variety of factors, such as sea level and climate change. Catastrophists contend that extinction happened suddenly. One catastrophic scenario is given above: an asteroid hurtles into earth setting in motion a series of events, including long periods of darkness and cold.

Scientists and the public have focussed particular attention on the extinction at the Cretaceous-Tertiary boundary—65 million years ago—which saw the demise of the dinosaurs.

The gradualists have pointed to a number of slow mechanisms, including climate change, competition from mammals, the evolution of inedible plants, and changes in sea level, to explain the disappearance of a group that dominated life on land for 140 million years. Paleontologists have observed that, at the end of the Cretaceous, tropical vegetation gradually, over 5 to 10 million years, gave way to conifer forest cover and some deciduous species better adapted to cooler conditions. These temperate conditions better suited the insulated, hot-blooded mammals and, in the end, led to the decline of the uninsulated, cold-blooded dinosaurs—assuming dinosaurs were cold-blooded. The deteriorating climate may have been linked to continental drift. The separation of the continents during the Cretaceous may have altered ocean currents and wind patterns, leading to generally cooler conditions. Massive volcanism that accompanied continental drift may also have contributed to a cooling trend.

Or did the cooling happen suddenly? Did the globe experience an asteroid-induced freeze or winter? This viewpoint was given a great boost in 1980 when a team led by California physicist Walter Alvarez discovered an iridium-rich layer of clay in limestone beds in Italy, exactly at the dividing line between the Cretaceous and the Tertiary. The beds contained 30 to 160 times the normal levels of this rare platinum-group element, which is found only in minute quantities in the Earth's crust. Iridium occurs at relatively enriched levels only in the Earth's underlying molten core or in extraterrestrial objects such as asteroids.

Studies subsequently showed iridium-rich layers at the Cretaceous-Tertiary boundary at 50 sites worldwide, seeming to confirm a cosmic catastrophe. Gradualists, however, maintained that massive volcanism, possibly associated with the Deccan traps in India, could account for the iridium and produce the climate-altering dust cloud.

Besides craters, asteroids leave other telltale signs. The intense heat and mechanical shock of impact produces glassy marbles (tektites) and shocked quartz crystals which bear characteristic herringbone patterns on their faces. But, gradualists say, massive volcanism can produce similar effects. As well, until recently, there has been no "smoking gun" to support the impact theory, that is, no known impact crater of Cretaceous-Tertiary age.

However, in 1991, a Canadian-led expedition found a crater, 175 kilometres (110 miles) wide, in Chicxulub on the Yucatan Peninsula in Mexico. It was of both the right age and dimension to support the asteroid impact theory for dinosaur extinction. The subsequent discovery, in Haiti, of tektites that could not have been produced by volcanism, and asteroid bits in the Western Pacific, Europe, New Zealand, the Atlantic and Indian Oceans, provided yet further support. The latter suggests that it may have been a meteor shower, rather than a single mass, that wiped out the dinosaurs 65 million years ago.

TRIASSIC-JURASSIC EXTINCTION

Considerably less attention has been focussed on the extinctions at the Triassic-Jurassic boundary. In some respects, this is surprising, for the extinction 200 million years ago was at least as large as the one at the Cretaceous-Tertiary boundary. Also, it is as important to the dinosaur story, for it heralds the rise of this fascinating group of animals.

The argument swirling around the Triassic-Jurassic extinction event is much the same as for that at the Cretaceous-Tertiary boundary: Did it happen slowly or suddenly? Those who argue for slow change point out that the global climate became increasingly hot and dry in the Late Triassic—the reverse of what happened at the end of the Cretaceous. These arid conditions favoured the reptiles rather than mammals. This may account for the demise of the once-dominant mammal-like reptiles, and the suppression of the true mammals. However, it is not obvious how modest early dinosaurs overcame their truly formidable archosaurian cousins. One explanation is that the more agile, early dinosaurs may have outcompeted the generally larger, but less mobile, archosaurs due to their superior upright form of locomotion.

Or did the dinosaurs merely get a lucky break in the form of an asteroid impact?

The discovery of the earliest Jurassic assemblage of animals at Wasson Bluff seems to provide a unique opportunity to examine this question. Survivors included small theropod dinosaurs, prosauropod dinosaurs, gracile crocodiles, sphenodontid reptiles, and mammal-like reptiles. Olsen calls it the "day-after community."

Due to the many lines of evidence in Fundy it is possible to date the extinction event very precisely. Preservation of the Wasson Bluff survivors occurred no more than a million years, and perhaps as few as 250 000 years, after the Triassic extinction—in geological terms, the day after. Even though hundreds of thousands of bones and footprints have been uncovered to date, there is no sign of the typical Triassic animals. Neither are there examples of new groups of animals. According to Olsen, "This pattern of only survivors is exactly the kind of transition that would be expected of a catastrophic extinction event such as that proposed for the Cretaceous-Tertiary boundary. One would not expect to find in the immediate aftermath of a catastrophe the origination of new families. Rather, day-after communities should be composed of survivors."

The presence of uniform lake cycles (Van Houten) in the Fundy Basin, either side of the T-J boundary, not only allows the very precise dating of the extinction event, it indicates that there was not a major environmental change that could account for the faunal changes.

The fact that there are diverse ancient environments represented at the Wasson Bluff site also strengthens the sudden extinction theory. "The nice thing in Nova Scotia," says Hans-Dieter Sues, now Associate Curator of Vertebrate Paleontology, Royal Ontario Museum, "is we have dune deposits, we have lake deposits, we have fluvial river deposits and all these show the same thing: that all the typical late Triassic forms are gone, and have given way to a completely different type of community. So, that gives us a great deal of confidence that

C h a p t e r   S i x

indeed there was a major biological change at the Triassic-Jurassic boundary. This kind of major change observed in many different environments cannot simply be explained away as chance sampling in a single odd environment."

One paleontologist countered that the extensive faulting and volcanism evident at Wasson Bluff might account for the killing-off of Triassic fauna. But testing has shown that the volcanism post-dates the boundary.

In the Fundy Basin, the T-J boundary occurs in the shales just below the North Mountain basalt. Sarah Fowell, a student of Olsen, investigated the change in plant life at the T-J boundary in the rocks at Partridge Island, near Parrsboro. What she found was a rapid and dramatic changeover from a high-diversity Triassic flora—conifers, ferns, cycads, and various extinct plants—to a low-diversity Jurassic plant community, dominated by the hardy coniferous cheirolepids. A similar change occurs within a very short period of time—a maximum of 20 000 years—at the T–J boundary in New Jersey. It is extremely unusual for a floral change to occur with such rapidity. The only other instance in the geological record where such a dramatic transition has been noted is at the Cretaceous-Tertiary boundary (K-T). "I think the kind of floral change we see in the Fundy Basin is consistent with an asteroid impact," says Olsen.

There is further evidence in New Jersey, where a fern spike occurs. This fern spike—the plant community is 90% ferns—is sandwiched exactly between Triassic-type and Jurassic-type plant communities, indicating that something unusual has happened. This sudden upswing in the proportion of ferns in the plant community is similar to what has been observed at the K-T boundary. Ferns are generally first colonizers of a disturbed environment. For example, when an island was born off Iceland in the 1960s the first thing to grow there were ferns; similarly, when Krakatoa exploded in the 19th century, ferns were the first plants to colonize its shores. "So ferns are the type of plant you'd get abundantly after a catastophe," says Olsen, the implication being that an asteroid impact would have laid waste to the land, and ferns would be the first sign of a recovering ecosystem.

This is circumstantial evidence, however. What is needed to confirm the theory is the discovery of shocked quartz. (Iridium only occurs if the asteroid itself was iridium-rich.) Olsen plans to continue the search for shocked quartz in the layers just under the fern spike in New Jersey. He will look in Nova Scotia as well, though conditions are not as ideal here.

Olsen would also like to find an asteroid impact crater of the correct age and size—the "smoking gun." The most promising candidate was the giant Manicouagan crater in northern Quebec. The original crater was 100 kilometres (62 miles) wide and must have been made by an asteroid 10 kilometre (6 miles) in diameter. It would have released energy equivalent to 10 000 times the force of the Earth's total arsenal of nuclear weapons, and could have precipitated a "nuclear winter." Radiometric dating of the Manicouagan crater, however, indicates an age of 214 ± 1 mya, which is too early to correlate with the extinction observed at Wasson Bluff precisely dated at 201 ± 1 mya. In 1992, however, an American team discovered shocked quartz in Italy, just at the Triassic-Jurassic boundary. The search for a meteor crater of the right age continues, keeping in mind that it took 14 years to find the Chicxulub Crater.

OUT WITH THE OLD, IN WITH THE NEW

The idea of sudden mass extinction as a force that shaped life on Earth is a radical one indeed. It poses serious challenges to the traditional model for change in the history of earth and life. Sir Charles Lyell first formulated these ideas, and Darwin later adapted them. Lyell said, "The present is the key to the past." If given enough time, he said, all phenomena could be explained by what you could observe going on around you today. Erosion of mountains or slow evolution of animals, for example.

The idea of asteroid impacts mounts a serious challenge to this Lyell-Darwinian view of the world, that change happens slowly. Apparently, sudden catastrophic change is also possible. Some eminent scientists, like Harvard paleontologist Stephen Jay Gould, believe that it is the most plausible explanation for the rapid turnovers of life observed in the fossil record. Extinction theorist David Raup, the author of *Extinction, Bad Genes or Bad Luck*, has observed: "Perhaps the past is actually the key to the present (and future)." Perhaps the dinosaurs did not die out because they were poorly adapted—bad genes—but because they were unlucky.

Perhaps, too, small is better when it comes to surviving catastrophic change. There is an intriguing similarity between the two extinctions that bracket the rise and fall of dinosaurs. All of the survivors at Wasson Bluff were relatively small. As well, no animal with a body weight greater than 25 kilograms (55 pounds) seems to have survived the Cretaceous-Tertiary boundary. This fits the impact theory for extinction. The immediate effects of the fireball and the longer-lasting collapse of photosynthesis would likely exterminate many larger life forms. Smaller animals would need less food and would reproduce more quickly. Also they were able to burrow or hibernate and therefore be more likely to survive the immediate aftermath of such an assault on the planet's life-support systems.

THE DAY AFTER

A new day dawns on the Jurassic in Nova Scotia. As the light streaks over top the Cobequids, it reveals a much more barren landscape than occupied the region in Triassic times. Volcanic activity has wrought a rugged, in places blackened, terrain. A shallow freshwater lake (playa) stretches out on the rift valley floor. A river meanders from the highlands toward the lake. But despite the watering of the landscape, this is now an arid setting dominated by large, Saharan-scale sand dunes.

Just as desert environments are now populated by reptiles, so, too, was Jurassic Nova Scotia. Sphenodontid reptiles scamper acoss the hot curves of the dunes. They search furtively for the sparse vegetation, cropping it with their parrot-like mouths. In places, basalt boulders have tumbled down from cliffs to form talus cones. As the sun and heat rises, the little reptiles will seek shelter there.

The trithelodont *Pachygenelus,* a mammal-like reptile

The boulders also provide protection from the fleet-footed crocodilian predators—sphenosuchids and protosuchids—which patrol the dunes. Bipedal, flesh-eating theropod dinosaurs also are on the prowl, either singly or in hunting packs. As the light of the new day dawns, nocturnal mammal-like reptiles seek safety in burrows or under brush, out of view of their reptilian predators.

Small herds of prosauropod dinosaurs march across the arid landscape in search of shrubby cheirolepids to browse. In the distance the saline lake shimmers—a mirage in the rising heat. Crocodilians and dinosaurs crisscross the muddy shores of the receding lake, leaving their footprints to bake in the hot sun.

Two hundred million years later, humans will find them— traces of a vanished world.

Hunting pack of
Early Jurassic
dinosaurs

CHAPTER SEVEN

MORE MARVELOUS CHAPTERS IN THE BIG VOLUME

"I never travelled in any country where my scientific pursuits were better understood or more zealously forwarded than in Nova Scotia."
SIR CHARLES LYELL,
TRAVELS IN NORTH AMERICA, 1842

ir Charles Lyell was already recognized as the founder of modern geology when he made his first visit to Nova Scotia in 1840. Even so, he was pleased, and a bit surprised, with the enthusiastic reception that he received. In Parrsboro he was met by the local country doctor, Abraham Gesner. Gesner was himself a seasoned scientist. He had authored the region's first treatise on geology, and later would earn lasting fame as the inventor of kerosene. Gesner guided his esteemed guest to Joggins. Lyell was duly impressed with "the subterranean forest" in the fossil cliffs, so much so, in fact, that he wrote in his *Travels in North America:* "I never enjoyed the reading of a marvellous chapter of the big volume more."

He would return a decade later and this time, in company with Sir William Dawson, "open a new chapter" in the big volume of geology with the discovery of the first terrestrial vertebrates inside the fossil trees. Sir William Logan, the first Director of the Geological Survey of Canada, himself already had added a chapter with the discovery of the first terrestrial footprints at Horton Bluff.

The seaside exposures in Fundy continued to draw fossil hunters to its shores throughout the 19th and 20th centuries. The discoveries of the 1980s added the missing chapter of the earliest Jurassic to the worldwide fossil record.

The good fortune that generations of fossil hunters have enjoyed on the shores of the Bay of Fundy is due in large part to the power of Fundy's famous 13.4 metre (44-foot) tides—the highest in the world. They will continue to erode the coastal cliffs, exposing new fossils and opening new windows in time.

"The area will yield important things for many years," says Hans-Dieter Sues of the Royal Ontario Museum.

It is interesting to speculate on what researchers might yet find. It is surprising that true mammals have not yet been found, for example, as they already existed in the early Jurassic along with their close relatives, the trithelodonts. As well, flying reptiles, the pterosaurs, flapped their leathery wings in the early Jurassic skies. Turtles, too, were well-established by that time, and fossils are abundant elsewhere—yet, not a scrap of turtle bone has been recovered in Fundy. Perhaps the largest omission is a complete absence of bones for large carnivorous dinosaurs, not only in Fundy, but in the whole of Eastern North America. Footprints made by large meat-eaters, such as *Eubrontes*, exist throughout the Newark Supergroup. Though it is uncommon to find tracks and bones together as they often require different conditions for preservation, in Fundy, hard fossils and trace fossils often exist side by side. So, the skeleton of a large carnivore—a truly "terrible lizard"—may yet come to light in the Fundy cliffs.

What future generations of fossil hunters find may well surprise the world as much as did the little reptile entombed in a fossil tree trunk at Joggins, or a whole community of early Jurassic creatures preserved in the cliffs at Wasson Bluff.

One thing seems certain: Fundy will contribute more marvellous chapters to the big volume.

The Fundy Geological Museum is designed to stimulate public interest in, and scientific research of, the important fossils found here. Just as Nova Scotia welcomed and fostered Lyell's ideas a century and a half ago, the province today wishes to advance the science of paleontology through the auspices of the Nova Scotia Museum.

In the past, important Fundy fossils were collected and removed from Nova Scotia for study in other parts of Canada, the United States, and Europe. Many of these fossils still reside in collections outside the province.

At the time, it was not against the law to remove fossils. However, in 1980, Nova Scotia passed the Special Places Protection Act to safeguard important historical, archaeological and paleontological sites. Removal of any fossil, or even disturbance of a fossil site, can result in the loss of important scientific knowledge. For this reason, the Act now makes it illegal to dig fossils or artifacts without a Heritage Research Permit.

The Nova Scotia Museum will continue to co-operate with visiting scientists who wish to seek and study Fundy's fossils. Any permit to remove fossils from the Province for study, however, is now issued on condition that they are eventually returned. It is hoped that fossils previously removed for study—many of which have been described in this book—will find a permanent home in the Fundy Geological Museum where they can be enjoyed by the public and be accessible to future generations of researchers.

BIBLIOGRAPHY

- Alvarez, L.W., Alvarez, W., Asaro, F., and Michel, H.V., 1980. *Extraterrestrial cause for the Cretaceous-Tertiary extinction.* Science, Vol. 208, Number 448, pp. 1095-1107.
- Ash, S., 1990 *Petrified forest, the story behind the scenery.* Petrified Forest Museum Association, Arizona.
- Bakker, R.T., 1986. *The dinosaur heresies.* William Morrow & Co., New York.
- Benton, M.J., 1991. *The rise of the mammals.* Quarto Publishing, London.
- Benton, M.J., 1989. *On the trail of the dinosaurs.* Quarto Publishing, London.
- Briggs, D.E.G., Plint, A.G., and Pickerill, R.K., 1984. *Arthropleura trails from the Westphalian of Eastern Canada.* Paleontology, Vol. 27, pp. 843-855.
- Campbell, W., 1992. *A Canadian scientist finds the smoking gun.* The Globe and Mail, November 7, 1992.
- Carroll, R.L., 1970. *The earliest known reptiles.* Yale Scientific Magazine, October 1970.
- Chronicle-Herald, The, 1988. *Fossil finds among oldest unearthed.* July 28, 1988.
- Colbert, E.H., 1984. *The great dinosaur hunters and their discoveries.* Dover Publications Inc., New York.
- Czerkas, S. J. and Czerkas, S.A., 1990. *Dinosaurs, a complete world history.* Dragon's World, Surrey.
- Dawson, J.W., 1891. *The geology of Nova Scotia, New Brunswick and Prince Edward Island or Acadian geology,* 4th ed. MacMillan & Co., London.
- Dawson, J.W., 1863. *Air breathers of the coal period.* Dawson Brothers, Montreal.
- Dixon, D., 1984. *The age of dinosaurs, a photographic record.* Methuen, Agincourt.
- Dodson, P., consultant, 1990. *Encyclopedia of dinosaurs.* Beekman House, New York.
- Ferguson, L., 1988. *The fossil cliffs of Joggins.* The Nova Scotia Museum, Halifax.

- Gesner, A., 1836. *Geology and Minerology of Nova Scotia.* Gossip and Coade, Halifax.

- Gillette, D.D. and Lockley, M.G., eds., 1989. *Dinosaur tracks and traces.* Cambridge University Press, Cambridge.

- Godfrey, S.J., Forillo, A.R., and Carroll, R.L., 1987. *A newly discovered skull of the temnospondyl amphibian Dendrerpeton acadianum Owen.* Canadian Journal Earth Sciences 24, pp. 796-805.

- Gould, S.J., ed., 1993. *The book of life.* Penguin Books, Toronto.

- Harrington, B.J., 1883. *The life of Sir William E. Logan.* Dawson Brothers, Montreal.

- Horner, J.R., and Gorman, J., 1990. *Digging Dinosaurs.* Harper and Row, New York.

- Lessem, D., 1992. *Kings of creation.* Simon & Schuster, New York.

- Lockley, M.G., 1986. *The paleobiological and paleoenvironmental importance of dinosaur footprints.* Palaios, Vol. 1, pp. 37-47.

- Lull, R.S., 1953. *Triassic Life of the Connecticut Valley.* State of Connecticut, State Geological and Natural History Survey, Bulletin No. 81.

- Lyell, C., 1845. *Travels in North America with geological observations on the United States, Canada, and Nova Scotia.* Murray, London.

- Midgley, R., Pring, E., and Wilhide, E., eds., 1983. *A field guide to dinosaurs.* Avon Books, New York.

- National Geographic Society, 1986. *Richest 200-million-year-old site of North American fossils found.* January 29, 1986.

- Norman, D., 1985. *The illustrated encyclopedia of dinosaurs.* Salamander Books, London.

- Olsen, P.E., Schlische, R.W., and Gore, P.J.W., 1989. *Tectonic, depositional, and paleoecological history of early Mesozoic rift basins, eastern North America.* Field Trip Guidebook T351, pp. 133-161.

- Olsen, P.E., Shubin, N.H., and Anders, M.H., 1987. *New early Jurassic tetrapod assemblages constrain Triassic-Jurassic tetrapod extinction event.* Science, 28 August 1987, pp. 1025-1029.

- Olsen, P.E., 1986. *Impact theory: Is the past the key to the future?* Lamont, 1985-1986. Lamont-Doherty Geological Observatory of Columbia University, Palisades.

- Olsen, P.E., 1986. *Discovery of earliest Jurassic reptile assemblages from Nova Scotia: imply catastrophic end to the Triassic.* Lamont Newsletter 12, Lamont-Doherty Geological Observatory of Columbia University, Spring 1986.

- Padian, K., ed., 1990. *The beginning of the age of dinosaurs, faunal changes across the Triassic-Jurassic boundary.* Cambridge University Press, Cambridge.

- Raup, D.M., 1991. *Extinction, bad luck or bad genes?* W.W. Norton & Co., New York.

- Raup, D.M. and Sepkoski, J.J., 1986. *Periodic extinction of families and genera.* Science, 21 February 1986.

- Reid, M., 1990. *The last great dinosaurs.* Red Deer College Press, Red Deer.

- Roberts, R., 1986. *Dinosaurs are forever.* Columbia, The Magazine of Columbia University, October, 1986.

- Russell, D.A., 1989. *An odyssey in time: the dinosaurs of North America.* University of Toronto Press, Toronto.

- Roland, A.E., 1982. *Geological background and physiography of Nova Scotia.* The Nova Scotia Museum, Halifax.

- Sarjeant, W.A.S. and Mossman, D.J., 1983. *The footprints of extinct animals.* Scientific American, Vol. 248, No. 1, pp. 75-85.

- Sargeant, W.A.S. and Mossman, D.J., 1978. *Vertebrate footprints from the Carboniferous sediments of Nova Scotia: a historical review and description of newly discovered forms.* Paleogeography, Paleoclimatology, Paleoecology, 23 (1978): 279-306.

- Sues, H., 1993. *A lucky break for dinosaurs.* Rotunda, Summer 1993, pp. 35-38.

- Thulborn, T., 1990. *Dinosaur tracks.* Chapman and Hall, London.

- Thurston, H., 1990. *Tidal life, a natural history of the Bay of Fundy.* Camden House, Camden East.

- Thurston, H., 1986. *The fossils of Fundy.* Atlantic Insight, July 1986.

- Wilford, J.W., 1986. *The riddle of the dinosaur.* Alfred J. Knopf, New York.

INDEX

91